Developing Effective Research Proposals

SAGE was founded in 1965 by Sara Miller McCune to support the dissemination of usable knowledge by publishing innovative and high-quality research and teaching content. Today, we publish over 900 journals, including those of more than 400 learned societies, more than 800 new books per year, and a growing range of library products including archives, data, case studies, reports, and video. SAGE remains majority-owned by our founder, and after Sara's lifetime will become owned by a charitable trust that secures our continued independence.

Los Angeles | London | New Delhi | Singapore | Washington DC | Melbourne

Developing Effective Research Proposals

3rd Edition

Keith F Punch

SAGE

Los Angeles | London | New Delhi
Singapore | Washington DC | Melbourne

Los Angeles | London | New Delhi
Singapore | Washington DC | Melbourne

SAGE Publications Ltd
1 Oliver's Yard
55 City Road
London EC1Y 1SP

SAGE Publications Inc.
2455 Teller Road
Thousand Oaks, California 91320

SAGE Publications India Pvt Ltd
B 1/I 1 Mohan Cooperative Industrial Area
Mathura Road
New Delhi 110 044

SAGE Publications Asia-Pacific Pte Ltd
3 Church Street
#10-04 Samsung Hub
Singapore 049483

Editor: Mila Steele
Editorial assistant: Alysha Owen
Production editor: Ian Antcliff
Marketing manager: Sally Ransom
Cover design: Shaun Mercier
Typeset by: C&M Digitals (P) Ltd, Chennai, India
Printed and bound by CPI Group (UK) Ltd,
Croydon, CR0 4YY

Library of Congress Control Number: 2015950624

British Library Cataloguing in Publication data

A catalogue record for this book is available from
the British Library

MIX
Paper from
responsible sources
FSC® C013604
www.fsc.org

ISBN 978-1-4739-1637-1
ISBN 978-1-4739-1638-8 (pbk)

At SAGE we take sustainability seriously. Most of our products are printed in the UK using FSC papers and boards.
When we print overseas we ensure sustainable papers are used as measured by the PREPS grading system.
We undertake an annual audit to monitor our sustainability.

CONTENTS

1
INTRODUCTION

1.1. RESEARCH PROPOSALS – PURPOSE AND USE OF THIS BOOK

The research proposal is a central feature of the research world. Typically, the presentation and approval of a formal proposal is required before a piece of research can proceed.

This applies to the graduate student in a university, for whom the research dissertation (or thesis) lies ahead, and for whom the approval of a research proposal is required in order to proceed with the dissertation. It applies also to the application for funds to support research, where the proposal is the vehicle by which the proposed research is assessed, and decisions are made about its funding.

This book is mainly written for the graduate student in the university, but I hope it will also be useful for other situations where proposals are required. Its central purpose is to help students develop research proposals, assuming that the research involved is **empirical** research in some area of **social science**. The idea of empirical research is discussed in Section 1.2.1. The ideas of social science, and of different social science areas which use empirical research, are discussed in Section 1.2.4.

To achieve its purpose, the book is organized around three central themes:

- What is a research proposal, who reads proposals and why (Chapter 2)?
- How can we go about developing a proposal? What general guidelines and strategies are there to help students, while recognising at the same time that the wide variety of social science research implies that we should not try to be too prescriptive or restrictive about this? This theme is subdivided into a general framework for developing proposals (Chapter 4), issues (Chapter 5), methods (Chapter 6) and tactics (Chapter 8).
- What might a finished proposal look like (Chapter 7)?

By way of introduction, I suggest a 'four Ps' view of the proposal – *phase*, *process*, *product*, *plan*:[1]

- The research proposal is a *phase* of the overall research process – the phase which launches the project, and therefore a very important first phase.
- Developing a research proposal is a *process* of planning, designing and setting up the research, including placing it in context and connecting it to relevant literature.
- The finished proposal is a *product*, where the proposal is formally presented as a document.
- That document contains the proposed *plan* for the execution of the research.

This description of the proposal suggests different ways you might read and use this book, choosing the chapters according to your interests and needs. For example, if your main interest is in the process of developing a proposal (how is it done?), I suggest you concentrate first on Chapters 2 and 8, then on Chapter 4, and then fit the other chapters in around these.

---

[1] I am indebted to Sandra Carrivick for this suggestion.

If your main interest is in the proposal as a finished product (what does it look like?), you might start with Chapter 7, then read Chapter 2 and then the other chapters as required. If you want to focus on the plan for the research (how will the research be done?), I suggest starting with Chapter 4, then proceeding to Chapters 6 and 7. If you want an overview of all of this, you might read the chapters in the order presented.

Section 1.4 gives more detail about the chapter plan for the book. The remainder of this chapter now gives some background to it.

1.2 BACKGROUND TO THIS BOOK

1.2.1 Empirical research – data

Our subject is empirical social science research, and developing proposals for doing such research. **Empiricism** is a philosophical term to describe the epistemological **theory** that regards experience as the foundation or source of knowledge (Aspin, 1995: 21). Since experience refers here to what is received through the senses, to sense-data or to what can be observed, I will use the general term 'observation' alongside the term 'experience'. Thus 'empirical' means based on direct experience or observation of the world. To say that a question is an empirical question is to say that we will answer it – or try to answer it – by obtaining direct, observable information from the world, rather than, for example, by theorising, or by reasoning, or by arguing from first principles. The key concept here is 'observable information about (some aspect of) the world'. The term used in research for this observable information about the world, or direct experience of the world, is **data**. The essential idea in empirical research is to use observable data as the way of answering questions, and of developing and testing ideas.

Empirical research is the main type of research in present-day social science, but it is not the only type. Examples of other types of research are theoretical research, analytical research, conceptual-philosophical research and historical research. This book concentrates on empirical research. At the same time, I believe many of the points it makes about proposal development can be applied to other types of research.

BOX 1.1

Types of research

Empirical research rests on empirical questions – questions which are answered using data. But there are other types of questions. One type is analytic. By this we mean that an analytic question can be answered by analysis of the question itself. An empirical question

(Continued)

(Continued)

requires empirical evidence – that is, data – in order to answer it. An analytic question, by contrast, can be answered by analysis of the question itself, without recourse to real-world data.

The nature of empirical questions is not hard to understand, partly because the scientific method, which is based on empiricism, saturates the modern (Western) world, so that empirical questions are everywhere. The nature of analytic questions can be harder to understand. Because they involve the analysis of concepts and propositions themselves the analysis is sometimes called analysis from first principles.

More generally, concepts, propositions and theories can be analysed, without necessarily involving empirical data, focussing on such things as their definitions, properties, implications and internal consistency. This is what is meant by such terms as analytical research, research from first principles, and theoretical and conceptual research. The point stressed here is that, while these types of research have their importance, they are different from empirical research.

Historical research is slightly different again. It concentrates on historical matters or phenomena, using the techniques of inquiry and analysis developed by historians. In one important sense, historical research is empirical, resting ultimately on real world data. Despite this, it is not usually seen as part of empirical social science research, because of the specialised issues that arise when dealing with data and phenomena from the past.

This book focuses on empirical research, easily the most important type of research in present day social science.

1.2.2   Quantitative and qualitative data

Data is obviously a very broad term, so we subdivide data for empirical research into two main types:

quantitative data – which are data in the form of numbers (or measurements), and

qualitative data – which are data not in the form of numbers (most of the time, though not always, this means words).

This leads to two simplifying definitions:

- **Quantitative research** is empirical research where the data are in the form of numbers.
- **Qualitative research** is empirical research where the data are not in the form of numbers.

These simplified definitions are useful for getting started in research, but they do not give the full picture of the quantitative–qualitative distinction. The term 'quantitative research' means more than just research which uses quantitative or numerical data. It also refers to a whole way of thinking, or an approach, which involves a collection or cluster of methods, as well as data in numerical form. Similarly, qualitative research is much more than just research which uses non-numerical data. It too is a way of thinking,[2] or an approach, which similarly involves a collection or cluster of methods, as well as data in non-numerical or qualitative form.

Thus, full definitions of the terms 'quantitative research' and 'qualitative research' would include:

- the way of thinking about the social reality being studied, the way of approaching it and conceptualising it;[3]
- the designs and methods used to represent that way of thinking, and to collect data;
- the data themselves – numbers for quantitative research, not numbers (mostly words) for qualitative research.

In teaching about research, I find it useful initially to approach the quantitative–qualitative distinction primarily through the third of these points, the nature of the data. Later, the distinction can be broadened to include the first two points – ways of conceptualizing the reality being studied, and methods. Also, I find that in the practical business of planning and doing research, dissertation students very often focus on such questions as: Will the data be numerical or not? Am I going to measure variables in this research, or not? Or, in other words, will my research be quantitative or qualitative?

For these reasons, I think that the nature of the data is at the heart of the distinction between quantitative and qualitative research, and that is why I start with the simplified definitions shown above. But we need also to remember that there is more to the distinction than this, as shown in the other two points above, and that qualitative research is much more diverse than quantitative research, in its ways of thinking, in its methods and in its data.

1.2.3   Relaxing the quantitative–qualitative distinction

The quantitative–qualitative distinction has been of major significance in social science research, and a basic organizing principle for the research methods literature, up until now.

---

[2]More accurately, qualitative research is a collection of ways of thinking about social reality. Whereas quantitative research is relatively homogeneous in its way of thinking, qualitative research is rather more heterogeneous.

[3]This is part of what is meant by the term **paradigm** (see Section 5.2), involving assumptions about the nature of the reality being studied. As an example, quantitative research typically conceptualizes the world in terms of variables (which can be measured) and studies relations between these variables. Qualitative research, by contrast, often studies cases and processes, rather than variables.

Despite that, we should note that the value of this sharp distinction has long been questioned in the literature (see, for example, Hammersley, 1992: 41–3), and that there are important similarities between the approaches.

Therefore, once understood, this distinction can be relaxed. This book deals with research proposals for both quantitative and qualitative studies, and is based on the view that neither approach is better than the other, that both are needed, that both have their strengths and weaknesses, and that they can and should be combined as appropriate. (Indeed, as pointed out in Section 1.2.5, it has become increasingly common to combine them, in what is now called **mixed methods**.)

Rather than either–or thinking about this distinction, or tired arguments about the superiority of one approach over the other, the viewpoint here is that the methods and data used (quantitative, qualitative or both) should follow from, and fit in with, the question(s) being asked. In particular, quantitative questions require quantitative methods and data to answer them, and qualitative questions require qualitative methods and data to answer them.

These statements are examples of the principle that questions and methods need to be matched with each other in a piece of research. In general, I believe that the best way to do this is to focus first on what we are trying to find out (the questions) before we focus on how we will do the research (the methods). This matter of question–method connections is discussed in Section 4.7.2.

1.2.4   Social science and social science areas

To call our research 'scientific', as in 'empirical social science research', requires that we see science as a method of inquiry and of building knowledge. There are different conceptions of science, but the one I suggest here is very general and widely applicable, has been prominent in the social sciences, and has great value in teaching research students.[4]

In this conception, the essence of science as a method is in two parts. One part concerns the central role of data. Science accepts the authority of empirical data – its questions are answered and its ideas are tested using data. The other part is the role of theory, particularly theory which explains (or explanatory theory). The aim is to explain the data, not just to collect the data and not just to use the data to describe situations or things. The two essential parts to science are therefore *data* and *theory*. Put simply, it is scientific to collect data about the world guided by research questions, to build theories to explain the data, and then to test those theories against further data. Whether data come before theory, or theory comes before data, is irrelevant. It only matters that both are present. There is nothing in this view of science about the nature of the empirical

---

[4]This view might be described as a 'modified logical empiricist' view, with some additions from critical rationalism (see Higgs, 1995).

data, and certainly nothing about whether the data are quantitative or qualitative. In other words, it is not a requirement of science that it involve numerical data, or measurements. It may well do so, but it is not necessary that it do so.

The general term 'social science' refers to the scientific study of human behaviour. 'Social' refers to people and their behaviour, and to the fact that so much of that behaviour occurs in a social context. 'Science' refers to the way that people and their behaviour are studied. If the aim of (all) science is to build explanatory theory about its data, the aim of social science is to build explanatory theory about people and their behaviour. This theory about human behaviour is to be based on, and tested against, real-world data.[5]

Together the social sciences cover a very wide domain, and we can distinguish between them in several ways. One distinction is between the basic social sciences (for example, sociology, psychology, anthropology) and the applied social sciences (for example, education, management, nursing). Behind this distinction is the idea that there are different perspectives (for example, individual or group) applied to different areas or settings. Despite the differences, however, one thing that unifies the social sciences is their focus on human behaviour, and the important role of empirical research in the way they are studied. Because of this central role of empirical research, a premise of this book is that there is a great deal of similarity in research methods across the various social science areas.

1.2.5   Relationship of this book to *Introduction to Social Research*

Two major developments in the last 40 years or so have greatly changed and broadened the field of research methods in the social sciences:

- The first development has been the growth of interest in, and the rapid development of, qualitative research methods, in many basic and applied social science areas. As a result, qualitative methods have moved much more into the mainstream of social science research, compared with their marginalized position of 40 years ago. They now sit alongside quantitative methods on a much more equal basis.
- The second development has been the rapid growth of mixed methods. This term describes empirical research methods which combine both qualitative and quantitative data and approaches. This second development has been a prominent feature of the field of research methodology since the late 1990s.

---

[5]In addition to explanation, another often-cited goal of empirical research into people and their behaviour is understanding. That is, rather than aiming for a set of propositions which together explain behaviour, researchers focus on understanding the behaviour, usually paying special attention to its context. This latter emphasis has a long history, and is usually traced back to the work of the German sociologist Max Weber in the nineteenth century. Interpretation, and 'the actor's definition of the situation', are typically central, and *interpretive research* is the name often given to this sort of inquiry. It tends to be qualitative in its methods.

Thus, the overall history of the main methodological developments in social science research can be conveniently described in terms of three waves:

- Wave 1 – the historical dominance of quantitative methods;
- Wave 2 – the emergence, acceptance and growth of qualitative methods;
- Wave 3 – the increasing tendency to combine quantitative and qualitative methods and data in mixed-method research.

In my opinion, this history means that researchers today need to understand the basic logic, characteristics and applicability of both quantitative and qualitative methods. For beginning researchers, I believe a firm foundation of understanding in both approaches is desirable, before any subsequent methodological specialization. It is also desirable that we reinforce the recent trends to move past the either–or thinking which characterized the quantitative–qualitative debate, and towards making full use of the two approaches.

Introduction to Social Research (Punch, 2011) aims to provide that foundation of understanding in both approaches. Its goal is to give an overview of the essentials of both quantitative and qualitative methods, set within a view of research which stresses the central role of research questions, and the logical priority of questions over methods. In this view, questions come before methods. We concentrate first on what we are trying to find out, and second on how we will do it. I see this view of research as pragmatic and robust. By 'pragmatic' I mean that it works, both in getting research started and getting it finished. By 'robust', I mean it works in a wide variety of situations and across many different areas.

Because *Introduction to Social Research* aims to be comprehensive, covering the essentials of both approaches for many social science areas, it does not go into details on some topics. The present book deals with the proposal development stage of research in much greater detail and in a much more hands-on way than was possible in *Introduction to Social Research*. It operates with the same model of research, and with the same view of quantitative and qualitative methods as is described in *Introduction to Social Research*, but it elaborates and develops issues and points about proposal development much further than was possible in that book.

1.3 A VIEW OF RESEARCH

Faced with the many definitions, descriptions and conceptions of research in the methodological literature, I think that it is sufficient for our present purposes to see research as an organized, systematic and logical process of inquiry, using empirical information to answer questions (or test hypotheses). Seen this way, it has much in common with how we find things out in everyday life – thus, the description of scientific research as 'organized common sense' is useful. Perhaps the main difference is the emphasis in research on being organized, systematic and logical.

This view of research, which I use as a teaching device, is shown in diagram form as Figure 2.1. It stresses the central role of research questions, and of systematically using empirical data to answer those questions. It has four main features:

- framing the research in terms of research questions;
- determining what data are necessary to answer those questions;
- designing research to collect and analyse those datà;
- using the data to answer the questions.

A modification of this model, to include hypothesis-testing research, is shown as Figure 4.1.

As well as capturing essential elements of the research process, I think this view also takes much of the mystery out of research, and enables students immediately to get started in planning research. It focuses on research questions, whereas some other writers focus on research problems. Whether to define the research in terms of questions or problems is a matter of choice for the researcher. The question–problem distinction in approaching research is discussed in Section 2.6.

1.4 CHAPTER OUTLINE

After this introductory chapter, Chapter 2 describes the proposal and its functions, and discusses who reads proposals and with what expectations. It then takes up the question–problem distinction, and presents the model of research referred to above. Chapter 3 deals with ethics in social science research. Chapter 4 provides a general framework for developing proposals, using this model of research and focusing on the central role of research questions. Chapter 5 discusses issues the researcher may need to consider concerning the roles of theory and of the literature, which arise because of the complexity of contemporary social science research methodology. Chapter 6 then moves on to consider the methods for the research, and Chapter 7 deals with the proposal as a finished product. Chapter 8 is concerned with the process of developing a research proposal and describes some tactics I have found useful working with students in proposal development. Chapter 8 includes five full proposals, and points to other examples of proposals in the literature. At the end of each of the first eight chapters, the main concepts discussed are brought together for review, and some exercises to assist in proposal development are given. A glossary of important terms completes the book.

1.5 REVIEW CONCEPTS

Empiricism A philosophy which sees observation and experience as the foundation of knowledge.

Empirical research Research which uses observable data to answer empirical research questions.

Quantitative data Empirical data in the form of numbers.

Qualitative data Empirical data not in the form of numbers (usually, this means data as words).

Quantitative research Empirical research where the data are in the form of numbers.

Qualitative research Empirical research where the data are not in the form of numbers.

Science As used here, a method of inquiry with the two central parts of empirical data, and theory.

Scientific research Research which uses the scientific method.

Social science Using the scientific method to study people and their behaviour.

Research questions Questions that empirical research aims to answer, using data.

2

UNDERSTANDING READERS, EXPECTATIONS AND FUNCTIONS

2.1 WHAT IS A RESEARCH PROPOSAL?

In one sense, the answer to the question 'what is a research proposal?' is obvious. The proposal for a piece of research is a document which deals with:

- what the proposed research is about;
- what it is trying to find out or achieve;
- how it will go about doing that;
- what we will learn from it and why that is worth learning.

After it is approved, the proposal leads to the project itself.

In another sense, the dividing line between the research proposal and the research project itself is not so obvious. The proposal describes what will be done, and the research itself is carried out after approval of the proposal. But preparing the proposal may also involve considerable research.

This is because the completed proposal is the *product* of a sustained *process* of planning and designing the research. And both the planning of the research and the proposal for the research are just as important as the phases of research which come after the proposal – those of executing and reporting the research. Indeed, in some types of research, especially those which are tightly preplanned (see Section 2.4), the planning of the research can be seen as the most critical phase of the process. In this sort of research, the plan which is developed forms the basis for the rest of the research.

Thus, the research proposal is a document which is the product of a process of planning and designing. As I will stress throughout this book, it is also an argument which needs to have a coherent line of reasoning and internal consistency.

Two other less obvious, but important, characteristics of the proposal are:

- The proposal is often the first time a researcher (especially a dissertation student) presents his/her work to some wider audience.
- As a finished product, it needs to be a 'stand-alone' document. This means that, at certain points in the approval process, it will be read by people who have not discussed the work with the researcher.

I return to these points later. To finish this section, I quote Krathwohl's (1998: 65) comprehensive definition of a research proposal:

> What is a proposal? It is an opportunity for you to present your idea and proposed actions for consideration in a shared decision-making situation. You, with all the integrity at your command, are helping those responsible for approving your proposal to see how you view the situation, how the idea fills a need, how it builds on what has been done before, how it will proceed, how you will avoid pitfalls, why pitfalls you have not

avoided are not a serious threat, what the study's consequences are likely to be, and what significance they are likely to have. It is not a sales job but a carefully prepared, enthusiastic, interestingly written, skilled presentation. Your presentation displays your ability to assemble the foregoing materials into an internally consistent chain of reasoning.

2.2   READERS AND EXPECTATIONS

There are two main situations where research proposals are required: the university context, where the issue is approval of the dissertation proposal for the research to proceed to enable the graduate student to complete the honours, master's or doctoral degree; and the research grant or funding context, where the issue is the competitive application for (usually scarce) research funds. Some of this goes on inside universities, but much of it happens outside universities.

As noted in Chapter 1, this book is written mainly with the graduate student in mind, who is preparing a research dissertation. As well as being a convenient way to organize and present the material about proposals, it is perhaps an area of greater need, because several books already exist to guide proposal writers in the research grant context (for example, Lauffer, 1983, 1984; Lefferts, 1982; Meador 1991; Miner and Griffith, 1993; Schumacher, 1992). But, while written mainly with the dissertation student in mind, much of what is said in this book applies to proposals in both contexts. And, as Kelly (2012) points out, the two contexts come together in the sense that social science graduates will have to apply their knowledge and earn their living in an increasingly competitive marketplace, so that practical skills such as proposal writing become important.

In the dissertation context, readers of the proposal (and members of dissertation committees or proposal review committees in particular) are required to make two sorts of judgements. First, there are judgements on a general level, which are concerned with the overall viability of the proposed study as a dissertation. Second, there are judgements on a more detailed and technical level, such as those concerned with the appropriateness of the research design, or quality control issues in data collection, or the proposed methods of data analysis. This section concerns judgements on the more general level.

The more general judgements centre on such questions as:

- Is the proposed research feasible and 'doable'?
- Is the research worth doing?
- Can the candidate do it?
- If done, will it produce a successful dissertation, at whatever level is involved?

In other words, review committees use the proposal to judge both the viability of the proposed research, and the ability of the candidate to carry it out. It is therefore a pivotal document in the dissertation student's journey. As Locke et al. (2011) point out:

In the context of graduate education the research proposal plays a role that reaches beyond its simple significance as a plan of action. In most instances the decision to permit the student to embark on a thesis or dissertation is made solely on the basis of that first formal document. The quality of writing in the proposal is likely to be used by advisors as a basis for judging the clarity of thought that has preceded the document, the degree of facility with which the study will be implemented if approved, and the adequacy of expository skills the student will bring to reporting the results. In sum, the proposal is the instrument through which faculty must judge whether there is a reasonable hope that the student can conduct any research project at all.

The four general questions listed above give a sense of the expectations readers are likely to have when they read the proposal, and of the general criteria they will use for judging it. Some of the implications for the proposal writer that follow immediately from those questions are:

- The reader needs to have sufficient information in the proposal to make the judgements shown above. The proposal needs to be thorough, and to address all necessary headings.

- The proposal needs to be clear, especially on what the research is trying to find out (or achieve), on how it will do that, on why it is worth doing, and on the context for the research.

- The proposal should show evidence of thorough and careful preparation, even when the research is of the less preplanned, more emerging kind. Research itself demands a systematic, thorough and careful approach, with attention to detail. The proposal should demonstrate, in its content and its presentation, that the student is aware of this.

- As noted already, the proposal needs to be a stand-alone document. This means that it needs to make sense to a reader, often non-expert, who has not discussed the work with the student, and who may not even know the student. The proposal should not need the student's presence to interpret or make clear what is being said.[1]

---

[1] I single this point out because of the frequency with which I find it occurs in research supervision. I am sure every supervisor is familiar with the following exchange:

Supervisor (reacting, for example, to a proposal draft): 'This is not clear', or 'I cannot understand this'.

Student (in response): 'What I meant was ...' and proceeds to clarify.

The point is, of course, that the student will usually not be there to clarify what is written when the committee member is reading the proposal, or when a wider audience is involved. It is necessary to make the proposal clear in the 'stand-alone' sense.

2.3 FUNCTIONS AND PURPOSE OF THE PROPOSAL

Locke et al. (2011) list three functions of the research proposal – communication, plan and contract. This section notes their comments on the communication and contract aspects of the proposal. Section 2.5 deals with the research proposal as a plan.

Communication The proposal communicates the investigator's intentions and research plans to those who give approval, or allocate funds. The document is the primary resource on which the graduate student's review panel (or dissertation committee) must base the functions of review, consultation and approval of the research project. It also serves a similar function for persons holding the purse strings of foundations or governmental funding agencies. The quality of assistance, the economy of consultation, and the probability of approval (or financial support) will all depend directly on the clarity and thoroughness of the proposal.

Contract In the research funding context, an approved grant proposal results in a contract between the investigator (and often the university) and a funding source. In the higher-degree context, an approved proposal constitutes a bond of agreement between the student and the advisers/supervisors, department or university. The approved proposal describes a study that, if conducted competently and completely, should provide the basis for a dissertation that would meet all standards for acceptability – a dissertation which should itself be approved. Accordingly, once the contract has been made, all but minor changes should occur only when arguments can be made for absolute necessity or compelling desirability (Locke et al., 2011). This idea of the proposal as contract is valuable, but this last statement needs modification for research which is more unfolding than prespecified. The distinction between prespecified and unfolding research is dealt with in Section 2.4 and again in Section 4.3 of this book.

Maxwell (2012) stresses that the form and structure of the proposal are tied to its purpose: 'to explain and justify your proposed study to an audience of non-experts on your topic'. *Explain* means that your readers can clearly understand what you want to do. *Justify* means that they not only understand what you plan to do, but why. *Your proposed study* means that the proposal should be mainly about your study, not mainly about the literature, your research topic in general or research methods in general. *Non-experts* means that researchers will often have readers reviewing their proposals who are not experts in the specific area.

2.4 PRESTRUCTURED VERSUS UNFOLDING RESEARCH

There is a difference between research which is **prestructured** (or preplanned or prefigured or predetermined) and research which is **unfolding** (or emerging or open-ended). The distinction, which has implications for proposal development, is about the amount of structure and specificity which is planned into the research.

More accurately, it is about the timing of such structure. The structure can be introduced in the planning or pre-empirical stage, as the proposal is being developed. Or it can emerge in the execution stage of the research, as the study is being carried out. Across the whole field of empirical social science research, studies may vary from tightly preplanned and prestructured to almost totally unfolding, with many positions in between. This is therefore a central issue to be clear about in planning the research, and in communicating that plan through the proposal. The distinction applies to the research questions, the design and the data, and it may also include the **conceptual framework**.

Research which is highly prestructured typically has clear and specific research questions, a clear conceptual framework, a preplanned design and precoded data. The clearest examples of prestructured studies come from quantitative research – experimental studies, and non-experimental quantitative studies with well-developed conceptual frameworks. On the other hand, research which is not prestructured typically does not have specific research questions which are clear in advance of the empirical work. A general approach is described rather than a tightly prefigured design, and data are not prestructured. These things will emerge or unfold as the study progresses. The clearest examples here are from qualitative research – an unfolding **case study**, an **ethnography**, or a life history.

These two descriptions represent the ends of a continuum. It is not a case of either–or, and varying degrees of prestructuring or unfolding are possible, as shown in Figure 4.1. When it comes to presentation of the proposal, it is likely that projects towards the left-hand end of this continuum will easier to describe – by definition, such research is highly preplanned, and the proposal describes that plan. Towards the right-hand end, the proposal writer has a different (and sometimes more difficult) problem. By definition, the proposal now cannot contain a detailed, highly specific plan. This is noted in the next section, and is discussed again in Sections 4.3 and 7.3.

2.5 THE RESEARCH PROPOSAL AS A PLAN

The proposal also serves as the action plan for carrying out the research. However, as noted above, how tightly preplanned the research is, and therefore how specific the plan in the proposal is, will vary across different research styles.

Much of the literature on proposals is relevant to research at the left-hand end of the structure continuum just described, and shown in Figure 4.1. Thus, Locke et al. (2011) describe tightly preplanned research when they write that empirical research:

consists of careful, systematic, and pre-planned observations of some restricted set of phenomena. The acceptability of results is judged exclusively in terms of the adequacy of the methods employed in making, recording, and interpreting the planned observations. Accordingly, the plan for observation, with its supporting arguments and explications, is the basis on which the thesis, dissertation or research report will be judged.

The research report can be no better than the plan of investigation. Hence, an adequate proposal sets forth the plan in step-by-step detail. The existence of a detailed plan that incorporates the most careful anticipation of problems to be confronted and contingent courses of action is the most powerful insurance against oversight or ill-considered choices during the execution phase of the investigation. The hallmark of a good proposal is a level of thoroughness and detail sufficient to permit the same planned observations with results not substantially different from those the author might obtain.

Similarly, Brink and Wood (1994: 236–7) are writing about highly prestructured research when they say that the plan is all-important, forming the basis for the remainder of the research process, and that developing the plan may well be the most critical part of the whole process. In this type of research, figuring out what you are going to do and how you are going to do it (that is, figuring out the plan) is the difficult part. Once that is done, all that is left to do is to 'do it' – to execute the preplanned steps.

These comments describe research which falls towards the left-hand end of the continuum shown in Figure 4.1. They need modification for those types of research which fall towards the right-hand end of the continuum. Proposals for unfolding studies are discussed in Sections 4.3 and 7.3.

2.6   RESEARCH QUESTIONS OR RESEARCH PROBLEMS?

Based on my experience in supervising research, I prefer to focus on the concept of research questions, as a generally useful way of helping students to get their research planning and proposal under way. When a student is having trouble getting started or making progress with the proposal, or is confused, overloaded or just stuck in developing it, one of the most helpful questions I can raise is 'What are we trying to find out here?' It is a short step from this to 'What questions is this research trying to answer?' or 'What are the research questions?' This approach makes *research questions* central.

By contrast, some writers tend to focus more on the 'problem behind the research', or on research problems, rather than on research questions. Thus, for Coley and Scheinberg (1990: 13) writing about proposal development in the human services context: 'Proposal writing includes the entire process of assessing the nature of the problem, developing solutions or programs to solve or contribute to solving the problem, and translating those into proposal format'. This approach makes the *research problem* central.

Other writers draw a sharp distinction between question and problem. Thus Locke et al. (2011), for example, arguing for 'semantic and conceptual hygiene', distinguish sharply between problem and question, and recommend a logical sequence of problem, question, purpose and hypothesis as the way forward in research planning and proposal development. Similarly, Brink and Wood (1994: 45) see proposal development as building or constructing the research problem, and see research question(s) as one of the central components of that. I think both of these frameworks are useful for highly preplanned research, and especially for intervention studies, but are less useful for more unfolding studies. In those cases, the distinction between problem and question is not so sharp.

Sometimes social research is concerned with interventions, and assessing their outcomes. Some areas of nursing research are a good example, especially those concerned with nursing in the clinical setting. Behind this focus on interventions lies the idea of a problem which needs a solution, and it is the intervention which is proposed as a solution (or part of a solution). This is the logic of the approach to proposal development described by Brink and Wood (1994) and by Tornquist (1993). Writing also about nursing, Tornquist describes research as intervention and action followed by evaluation and assessment. Similarly, programs and interventions in education or management might be driven by the same logic – a problem requiring a solution, which takes the form of an intervention. The research then becomes an evaluation or assessment of the effects of the intervention.

This line of thinking concentrates on the identification of a problem – something requiring a solution – followed by an intervention or activity designed to solve it, and the research becomes the assessment or evaluation of that intervention. Another, more general, line of thinking concentrates on the identification of question(s) – something requiring an answer – followed by an investigation designed to collect the data to answer the question(s).

In intervention research, the intervention is designed to solve or change some unsatisfactory situation. This unsatisfactory situation is the problem. On the other hand, thinking about research in terms of research questions is a more general approach, which can be used in naturalistic[2] research as well as in intervention research (the effects of an intervention can always be assessed through a series of research questions), and in basic research as well as applied research. I use the focus on research questions as a way both of getting started in research, and of organizing the subsequent project. I think it also has the benefits of reinforcing the 'question first, methods later' advice of Section 4.7.2, and of flexibility, in the sense that students often find it easier to generate research questions

---

[2]'Naturalistic' refers here to research which does not contrive or manipulate the situation being studied, and which does not involve any intervention or treatment. It studies the world 'as it is'.

than to focus on a problem. But if it helps to think in terms of identifying a research problem, rather than identifying research questions, there is no reason at all not to do so. Nor is there any reason not to use both concepts – problems and questions – and to switch between them as appropriate, in developing and presenting the proposal. In any case, there is interchangeability between the two concepts. Thus, a problem, as something requiring a solution, can always be phrased as questions. Likewise, a question, as something requiring an answer, can always be phrased as a problem.

It follows from this that an effective way to develop and present a proposal ties together the three concepts of problem, purpose and research questions. The purpose is the overall intention of the research. It proceeds from some problem which needs attention or solution. It is achieved by answering a set of research questions. This set of concepts has a convincing logical structure, and will be described again in Chapter 4.

2.7   A SIMPLIFIED MODEL OF RESEARCH

My focus on research questions, as a useful tool and strategy for developing proposals, leads to a simple but effective model of the research process. When the research is organized around research questions, and when each question conforms to the **empirical criterion** described in Section 4.6, we have the model of research shown in Figure 2.1.

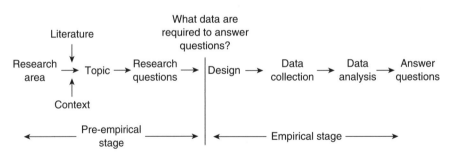

Figure 2.1   Simplified model of research (without hypotheses)

This simplified model of research stresses:

- framing the research in terms of research questions;
- determining what data are necessary to answer those questions;
- designing research to collect and analyse those data;
- using the data (and the results of the data analysis) to answer the questions.

This version of the model shows research questions without hypotheses. In Chapter 4, we consider the issue of hypotheses in the proposal. Where hypotheses are appropriate, this model can easily be modified to include them. The expanded model is shown as Figure 4.1.

Based on this model of research, we can see that two overall questions guide the research planning process. They are also the questions around which the research proposal can be written, and, later and with some additions, the dissertation (or research report). The questions are the straightforward ones of *what* (What questions is the research trying to answer?) and *how* (How will the research answer these questions?). Chapter 4 deals with ways of answering the 'what' question. Chapter 6 concentrates on the 'how' question, the question of methods. There is also a third question, the *why* question (Why are these questions worth answering? Why is this research worth doing?). This concerns the justification for doing the research, and is discussed in Chapter 7.

This model of research helps to organize the research proposal. During planning, it also helps to counter overload and possible confusion. It is effective with quantitative, qualitative and mixed-method research. It needs modification where prespecified research questions are not possible or desirable, and where the plan for the research is that they will be developed as the early empirical work provides focus. In those cases, it is still worth keeping this model in mind, in order to see where and why it is not appropriate. When research questions are developed as the research becomes focused, the analytic process is delayed. It comes during and after some empirical work, not before. When that happens, development of the research questions will be influenced by insights and trends emerging from the initial data. Otherwise, it is much the same process, and just as important for ensuring the fit between the parts of the research. This model is also effective with research conceptualized in terms of problems rather than questions. If the research is the assessment of an intervention designed as a solution to some problem, the assessment or evaluation can easily be structured as a series of research questions.

2.8 REVIEW CONCEPTS

Prestructured research Research which is carefully and thoroughly preplanned; has clear and specific research questions; typically also has a preplanned design, and precoded data; most typical of quantitative studies.

Unfolding research Research which is not so thoroughly preplanned; starting research questions are more general; uses a general approach rather than a tightly prefigured design; specific questions, and aspects of design emerge and are clarified as the study progresses; typical of some qualitative research.

——— EXERCISES AND STUDY QUESTIONS ———

Make sure you can answer these questions.

- Who will read my proposal?
- What will their expectations be?
- What is the process for approval of my proposal?
- What departmental and/or university guidelines are there for my proposal and its presentation?

3

INCLUDING ETHICS IN SOCIAL SCIENCE RESEARCH

ALIS OANCEA

3.1 THE IMPORTANCE OF ETHICS

There is a strong and still growing concern for ethical issues in social research today, stimulated by the growth in the use of qualitative methods. All research has ethical dimensions, and a good starting point for dealing with the ethical issues in the proposal is to realize that there are numerous stakeholders in your research. In addition to yourself, these include your supervisor(s), your university, your participants, and your examiners and other readers. Your goal should be to complete your dissertation with you and your university in good standing with your participants, and with your findings contributing to the advancement of knowledge or of professional practice (Steane, 2004: 59).

A researcher's ethical responsibilities include the overarching principles of academic integrity and honesty, and respect for other people. In developing a proposal, they include thinking through the ethical issues involved in your particular project, knowing and complying with your university's requirements regarding ethical issues, and writing your proposal (and, ultimately, your dissertation) with ethical issues in mind.

Ethical issues in planning and executing the research centre on access, consent and participants' protection. Since researchers cannot demand access to people, situations or data for research purposes, assistance and permission are necessarily involved. Thus, if the overall integrity, quality and worthiness of the research are conveyed by the proposal itself, important ethical issues to be considered, and the questions central to them, are:

- Informed consent. Do the people I wish to study have full information about the research, including why and how they have been chosen to participate? Is their consent freely given? What about if children are involved? Rudestam and Newton (2014) list 11 elements of informed consent, and Steane (2004: 64) points out that informed consent is not always a straightforward issue, especially in qualitative research. Bell (2014: 46–7) has a useful checklist for negotiating access, which includes some of the common ethical issues in social research.
- Confidentiality and anonymity. How will the information be safeguarded and the identity of people or institutions protected? How will anonymity be preserved, for people and institutions? Much of the discussion in the research ethics literature concerns personal confidentiality, but Le Voi (2002: 155) points out that commercial confidentiality may also be involved, as when research is carried out with the cooperation or sponsorship of commercial organizations. The same point applies to professional organizations.
- Ownership of data and conclusion. After collection and analysis, who owns the data and the conclusions? How will the research results be reported and disseminated?
- Use and misuse of results. What obligations do I have to help my findings be used appropriately, and not to be misused? (Miles et al., 2014).
- Honesty and trust. What is my relationship with the people I am studying?
- Reciprocity. What do participants gain from my research?

- Intervention and advocacy. What do I do if I see harmful, illegal, wrongful behaviour during my research?
- Harm and risk. What might this research do to hurt the people involved? Health and safety issues can be involved in some types of research, and in all cases, the principle of non-maleficence (no harm) takes precedence.
- Conflict of interest. Steane (2004: 66) points out that questions of power and reliance, along with benefit and trust, are involved in some research situations, and need to be handled with care.

Ethical issues are also involved in academic writing, and acknowledging the work of others is part of academic honesty and integrity. In particular, plagiarism, defined as 'fraudulently presenting ideas as your own when they are not' (Le Voi, 2002: 155), is to be avoided. The academic writer should also strive for bias-free writing, with no discrimination against or oppression of any group of people implied in the language or materials used. Rudestam and Newton (2014) have several useful tips for avoiding bias in writing.

In most situations today, the submission of a research proposal requires a completed ethics checklist, which may have a separate format. It is especially important, therefore, that you check practices, guidelines and requirements on this matter in your department and university.

Ethics is the study of what are good, right, or virtuous courses of action; applied ethics focuses this study on particular and complex issues and contexts. Research ethics is a branch of applied ethics focused on the specific contexts of planning, conducting, communicating and following up research. The study of these contexts and of the ethical aspects of the complex judgements that they require has produced a vast literature that sets out a range of values, general principles and specific rules to guide research practice, and explores the ways in which particular contexts shape ethical decision-making in research.

Some of these principles have been formalized into codes of ethical practice, which signal developing areas of consensus within communities of research about what is acceptable to do, in what conditions. For example, the codes may prompt researchers to consider issues of access and consent, of confidentiality and anonymity, or of risks and benefits in research, in light of recommendations based on moral principles, experience in the field, and insights from historical and ongoing debates around research ethics. Some of these areas of agreement have been further institutionalized to produce ethical regulations consisting of sets of procedural requirements for researchers (for example, for obtaining the approval of an ethics committee) deemed important by organizations involved in the scrutiny of research practice, including higher education institutions and funders of research.

Ethical challenges in research with people arise in all designs and approaches and at all stages of a project, from the choice of research topic, which raises questions about the worthwhileness of the research, through to the reporting and publication stage, and beyond it, to further uses and outcomes. The standard approach to research ethics involves a deductive move from principles and rules towards application. For example, in the context of the scrutiny of research proposals by institutional ethics committees, reviewers may identify a relevant rule (such as 'harm ought to be avoided') and use the relevant descriptive information about the proposed conduct of research to decide whether in the particular project under scrutiny the rule is likely to be infringed or not. This approach has been criticized by scholars who noted that principles and rules underdetermine practice, which is open-ended and situated (see McNamee and Bridges, 2002). Further, beyond ethical principles there can be many other constraints on ethical decision-making, such as legal, methodological, political, and economic considerations, which may shape research ethics procedures.

Social science researchers need to be alert to the various constraints around their research and to the ethical implications of any decisions they make. They engage in principled deliberation about morally salient issues and acceptable courses of action in particular research situations. In doing so, they can draw on their understanding of the particulars of each situation and of the personal and professional values infusing it, as well as on their critical interpretation of the regulation and various guidelines available to them.

3.2 ETHICAL PRINCIPLES AND RESEARCH SITUATIONS

Let us take a hypothetical example of an ethically rich research situation. A student wishes to study effective teaching practices in higher education. Having reviewed the literature, the student is concerned about two aspects of previous research: the potential for researcher-introduced bias and, linked to this, what she sees as an insufficient focus on power relations in the classroom. In an attempt to reduce bias and to uncover power relations in the classroom, she is considering doing covert observational research in her own higher education institution. She hopes not only to produce a trustworthy account of naturally occurring situations, but also an authentic account that can help empower participants who may be disadvantaged by the balance of power in such situations, including women and minority ethnic participants. Would covert research in this scenario be ethically acceptable?

Regardless of how accurate the hypothetical student's assessment of the literature seems, and of how realistic her expectations might be, this example invites the reader to engage in a form of 'normative' reasoning that involves statements about what ought to be done and why. This form of reasoning draws on factual statements about what is the case in a particular situation, and connects them with belief statements concerning aims, rules and principles about how things ought to be. The basic difference between thinking about (for example) how to achieve technically precise data collection and analysis, and deliberating about acting responsibly in ethically complex research situations is crucial in understanding the ethical context for research, researchers' responsibilities within it, and the resources available to help them navigate their way through it. What this distinction suggests is that, although factual statements about research, codes and guidelines, and rules of thumb are of help, ethical research practice is ultimately a matter of responsible, situated judgement.

So how might the student who is considering doing covert research in her own institution reason? There is no absolutely straightforward answer. Institutional guidelines may simply state that unjustified deception should be avoided, and leave it more or less to the researcher to construct a case for what may count as justified or reasonable deception. In philosophical ethics there are many traditions that may assist in this process, each of which may help illuminate a slightly different set of ethically salient aspects of research situations.

For example, the student could argue that her decision will have to be based on a trade-off in the application of different moral rules and principles. She could argue that 'do not deceive' is a lower-priority rule in a situation of perceived discrimination than 'maximize benefits for those who most need them'. Nonetheless, she could also, equally, argue that morally right aims do not justify morally wrong means, and therefore that there are no reasonable grounds for the decision to deceive.

To settle this dilemma, she may appeal to higher-order principles, such as the imperative to treat others with respect, or to exemplars of past moral behaviour, on which to model her own. The decision is ultimately hers, although it may draw on professional consensus crystallized in professional ethical codes and it may have been sanctioned by relevant committees and informed by debates within research communities. She also bears the moral – though perhaps not always, or not solely, the legal – responsibility for the consequences of her choice.

The example above looked at deception. We can interrogate other hypothetical situations in similar ways. For instance, is it acceptable to withhold benefits from participants in experimental research, if the control group is not offered a comparable alternative to the potentially beneficial treatment received by the intervention group? Also, in a different model of research, what should the researcher do when evidence of dangerous behaviour transpires from confidential interviews during the course of research?

In order to reach a decision about whether a particular way of conducting research would be acceptable in a concrete situation, the researcher needs to find ways to interrogate the situation and deliberate about her aims and the means by which they will be achieved, in the light of empirical information, ethical principles and rules of thumb, exemplars of action, and individual and collective moral and professional aspirations.

Box 3.1 illustrates three ways in which we could start to interrogate an ethically complex research scenario, each pointing to somewhat different ethical aspects and drawing on particular traditions in philosophical ethics. These show that there can be a range of focal points for thinking about ethics in research (but note that there are also many hybrid approaches that cut across particular traditions).

BOX 3.1

Interrogating Research Practice from a Range of Ethical Perspectives

1. Duties: What is my/my colleagues' duty to do in this situation? What is the right thing to do in this case? Have errors been made deliberately or due to negligence? How can these be reversed or corrected?
2. Consequences: What are the likely consequences of the courses of action available to me (including not doing anything)? How will each potential course of action affect the relevant individuals and communities (including myself) in this situation? What potential harms may result from each of these courses of action? What would be the benefits of different courses of action I might take? How do these different risks and benefits compare with each other? On balance, what is the best course of action to take now?
3. Virtues: How would a virtuous person act in this situation? Which values do I want to express in my action? How would my moral exemplars act in this situation? How should I live – what kind of person do I strive to be? Who do I want to be throughout this situation?

The first set of questions in Box 3.1 focuses on the ideas of duty, obligations and rights, and prompts the researcher to think about identifying the *right* course of action in the particular situation described. The questions reflect a long-standing tradition in ethics that many call *deontological* ethics (from the Greek *deon*, meaning duty), which emphasizes acting out of duty, as opposed to pleasure, inclination, or interest. This approach centres on universal principles (which hold irrespective of particular conditions); an example is Immanuel Kant's categorical imperative, one formulation of which states 'act in such a way that you always treat humanity, whether in your own person or in the person of any other, never simply as a means, but always at the same time as an end' (Kant, 1964: 96). In this tradition, ethical decision-making tends to be deductive: it starts with principles (such as truthfulness, respect, and beneficence), from which derive rules (such as 'do not deliberately distort your data', 'do not deceive', 'do not cause harm to participants'). Actual judgements refer to these rules, which are binding regardless of consequences. Deontological ethical approaches work well if there is a stock of rules based on absolute principles and values; if these rules are fair and widely accepted; if individuals and groups are prepared to uphold them regardless of immediate consequences; and if individuals and groups have access to guidance for the selection and application of rules, particularly in cases of conflict (such as possible conflict between truthfulness and beneficence).

The second set of questions in Box 3.1 focuses on the consequences of actions, and on the balance of benefits and harms arising from them. It aims to find the *best* course of action, that is, the one likely to result in the greatest good for all concerned. In *teleological* ethics (from Greek *telos* – aim, purpose, end, destination), the focus shifts from duty and universals to the outcomes or results of actions. Moral worth is determined by the consequences of an act; the nature of the act comes second to that. Good action aims to achieve the greatest good (health, happiness, welfare, knowledge) overall. This is the so-called 'greatest happiness' or utility principle: 'actions are right in proportion as they tend to promote happiness, wrong as they tend to produce the reverse of happiness' (Mill, 1863: 9–10). Other versions include achieving 'the greatest happiness of the greatest number' of people (Bentham, 1823: 9), 'the greatest possible balance of good over evil in the world' (Frankena, 1973: 34); maximizing benefits and minimizing harm for all those foreseeably affected by an action; and ensuring that action, including research, has a reasonable likelihood of bringing about benefits and that no alternative of comparable effectiveness exists (Declaration of Helsinki, Art. 19). Consequence ethics requires comprehensive understanding of the facts of the situation, accurate prediction of likely consequences, and the ability to ensure justice while maximizing good over harm.

The final set of questions moves away from the emphasis on universal principles and consequences towards actions arising out of particular dispositions in particular situations. The questions prompt scrutiny of one's own and others' ways of being and seek those dispositions or traits that embody moral excellence, or virtue, through their action. In other words, these questions seek the most *virtuous* ways of being and living. For *aretaic* ethics (from the Greek *arete* – virtue, value, excellence), acting ethically means acting in accordance with the traits, or dispositions, of the virtuous person. These may include intellectual impartiality, benevolence, honesty, or may refer to a more holistic concept of integrity and excellence in research. Virtuous action is based on moral wisdom and discernment, which includes an appreciation of the situation – that is, the capacity to understand the situation and to discern its morally salient issues. It is also an exercise of virtuosity – the skilful transposition of these dispositions into morally appropriate action. Ethically sound research cultures support virtuous research practice and the flourishing of virtuous researchers. There is no one principle or code to capture all this; at best, we only have rules of thumb and the examples of others to help us recognize, choose and sustain virtuous research. Thus, an aretaic approach is premised on the ability to recognize, understand and choose virtue, together with finely tuned, sensitive reading(s) of the situation, including understanding of the self and of others.

Other approaches to research ethics also stress the importance of particular situations in defining and addressing ethical issues. Situated ethical approaches emphasize that ethical decisions are contextual and ethical problems are never neatly defined, nor fully resolved. They show that ethical concerns in research, like more general ethical debates in society, are more wide-ranging than can be covered by sets of rules. Applied feminist ethics has a sharp focus on the key themes of power, responsibility and accountability and questions the notion of neutral expertise and the meaningfulness of ethical prescription that discounts standpoint, personal experience, emotion, nurturing, and caring (Edwards and Mauthner, 2002; Usher, in Simons and Usher, 2000).

3.3 PROCEDURAL REQUIREMENTS: THE ROLE OF ETHICAL CODES

Debates around ethics in research have a long history, but became more intense in the twentieth century. These debates were fuelled by scandals around harmful and exploitative studies, in particular in medical research, such as the Tuskegee syphilis study on black males, the Willowbrook School hepatitis study on disabled children, and many horrific **experiments** on humans during the Second World War and the Cold War. Psychological and social research entered the fray too – for example, the Iowa stuttering study on orphan children, the Stanford prison experiment, and the Milgram (1974) experiments on obedience were subject to intense controversy. Reactions to such experiments led to the establishment of formal regulation on research ethics, such as the 1947 Nuremberg code, the 1964 Helsinki Declaration by the World Medical Association, the 1979 Belmont Report in the USA, and a series of data protection and human experimentation acts worldwide. While many of the issues that were seen as controversial at the time of these debates would now be seen as unacceptable research practice, there are new difficult issues that have emerged since, as technologies available to researchers have become more complex. This has led to the development of new areas of research ethics (such as the ethics of geoengineering, virtual reality, stem cell, or human enhancement research), but also to challenging areas of past consensus (such as those around research with disabled subjects). Thus research ethics continues to be a dynamic field.

Professional regulations and ethical codes, including those for research, tend to include detailed rules that are more specific and limited in scope than the philosophical principles that may be underpinning them. They may draw unevenly on different ethical traditions, often in favour of a deontological approach. They stipulate standards for conduct or 'proper' ways of behaving for members of a profession, as well as a range of conditions and procedures for their application. These standards, such as those concerning informed consent and confidentiality, are the product of negotiated agreement about acceptable practice in particular professional, occupational and institutional contexts. They add collective and institutional dimensions to ethical decision-making in research. Their role is to offer resources that can inform ethically acceptable decisions by researchers; and to construct frameworks of consensus against which proposed and actual courses of action and research conduct can be judged and sanctioned by relevant bodies (for example, a committee granting or refusing 'ethical clearance', or an examiner deeming the approach described in a thesis as ethically acceptable or not). At the institutional level, the establishment of formalized mechanisms for ethical scrutiny also arises from a concern about litigation.

By way of example, Box 3.2 describes some of the better-known codes produced by professional associations and funding bodies in the field of educational research. Some of their prescriptions are especially stringent, as well as challenging, in research involving vulnerable populations, including children (defined in the United Nations Convention on the Rights of the Child as any person under the age of 18).

--- **BOX 3.2** ---

Ethical Codes and Regulation for Educational Research

The Australian Association for Research in Education's code of ethics (2005, http://www. aare.edu.au/pages/aare-code-of-ethics.html) starts with detailed statements of principles, drawn eclectically from a range of ethical traditions. These principles include: consideration of the extent to which the consequences of research enhance general welfare; recognition of the variety of views about what counts as a good life and, thus, as educationally worthwhile; and prioritizing respect for the dignity, worth and welfare of persons over considerations of public benefit or researchers' interests. The code then concentrates on procedural issues around minimizing harm, informed consent and voluntary participation, confidentiality, integrity and social responsibility in carrying out, reporting and publishing research.

The American Educational Research Association's code (2011, http://www.aera. net/Portals/38/docs/About_AERA/CodeOfEthics(1).pdf) draws on principles of professional competence, integrity, responsibility and respect for people's rights, dignity and diversity. It seeks to set standards for different stages and contexts of research, from research planning to publication and use. The standards include academic practice (for example, competence and training, contractual issues, conflicts of interests, publication and reviewing, authorship, and academic integrity) and stipulate in great detail the conditions for ensuring informed consent and confidentiality.

The ethical guidelines of the British Educational Research Association (2011, https://www.bera.ac.uk/wp-content/uploads/2014/02/BERA-Ethical-Guidelines-2011.pdf) state the association's commitment to 'an ethic of respect for the person, knowledge, democratic values, the quality of educational research, and academic freedom'. They describe procedural requirements in terms of researchers' responsibilities: to research participants (such as ensuring voluntary informed consent, privacy, the right to withdraw, and avoiding detriment); to sponsors of research; to the community of educational researchers (including appropriate conduct and recognition of authorship); and to educational professionals, policy-makers and the general public.

Finally, various funding bodies have also issued ethical standards, which can be highly prescriptive – they go beyond signalling professional values and function as ethical regulation. The UK's Economic and Social Research Council's ethics framework (2012, http://www.esrc.ac.uk/_images/Framework-for-Research-Ethics_tcm8-4586.pdf) opens with a statement of six 'principles', which are a mixture of moral principles and procedural requirements. It then provides a detailed technical description of ethical procedures and minimum requirements for funded projects. Similarly, the European Commission (http://cordis.europa.eu/fp7/ethics_en.html) has developed an ethical framework that combines a concern for the principles of respect for human dignity, utility, precaution and justice with detailed legal and technical requirements.

3.4 CHALLENGES IN SOCIAL SCIENCE RESEARCH ETHICS

Punch (1994) summarizes the main ethical issues in social research as harm, consent, deception, privacy and confidentiality of data. Miles and Huberman (2014 have a broader list of 11 ethical issues that typically need attention before, during and after qualitative studies, though many apply to quantitative studies also. Their list includes:

Issues arising early in a research project: the worthiness of the project; competence to carry out the project; informed consent; benefits, costs and reciprocity;

Issues arising as the project develops: harm and risk; honesty and trust; privacy, confidentiality and anonymity; intervention (for example, when wrongful or illegal behaviour is witnessed) and advocacy (for example, for participants' interests);

Issues arising later in, or after, the project: research integrity and quality; ownership of data and conclusions; use and misuse of results.

More recently, Hammersley and Traianou (2012) focus their discussion on the following concerns: risk of harm; autonomy and informed consent; and privacy, confidentiality and anonymity. At the same time, they warn against the dangers of what they see as excessive 'moralism', or 'overdoing' ethics in research (p. 136): they see ethics as a set of values extrinsic to the researchers' core task, which is one of producing knowledge 'in ways that answer worthwhile questions to the required level of likely validity' (pp. 1–2). They recommend a primary focus on 'intrinsic' research virtues, such as objectivity, independence, and dedication, as a way to resolve potential tensions between moral values and knowledge aims, or between 'virtue and validity' in research (Figueroa, in Simons and Usher, 2000: 82).

This section discusses some of the most common requirements placed upon university-based research and highlights some of the ethical challenges in conducting research in social science settings. The discussion focuses on requirements and procedures for the treatment of participants, arising from principles of autonomy, confidentiality and beneficence. Further requirements, such as those concerning academic conduct and misconduct (falsification, plagiarism, exploitation, discrimination, unacceptable publication practice, conflict of interests, etc.), are not discussed here, but are covered at length in the ethical codes described in Box 3.2.

3.4.1 Autonomy

Access to a research setting and/or to secondary data is normally negotiated with relevant gatekeepers (for example, a headteacher in a school). Responsible gatekeeping involves understanding research, sensitivity to the setting, and care for the participants. For their part, researchers need to be aware of the complexities of gatekeepers' positions (Homan, 2004). A headteacher, for example, may have to take many factors into account when faced with a request for access to her school, in order to prioritize between competing demands on pupils' and teachers' time.

EXAMPLE 3.1

Challenges of Access and Consent

On gaining access to teacher job interviews I reached an agreement with the head whereby he would either introduce me to all candidates or he will give me an opening to do this for myself. However, I soon found out that this rarely happened in a systematic way. In the first job interviews that I sat in on the head gave me an opportunity to introduce myself to candidates and to ask if they had any objections to me being present. Needless to say, neither of the candidates indicated any objection nor for that matter have any candidates since. However, it is dubious whether this kind of situation can be regarded as constituting informed consent given the power relations involved in the situation. What candidate would risk having me ejected from an interview when it was apparent that the head and the governors had invited me into the situation? (Burgess, 1989: 60)

Read Burgess's (1983) book, *Experiencing Comprehensive Education*.

After access to a setting, the collection of primary data is normally carried out with the explicit consent of participants, or of their legal representatives, in the case of populations where the likelihood of direct consent is questionable, as in the case of children. This requirement is usually termed 'voluntary informed consent', meaning that participants agree freely to be part of research, that they understand what their participation entails and how it will be reported, and that they feel free to withdraw their agreement at any time throughout the research process. Consent can be given actively, through opt-in procedures (such as when participants actively sign and return a consent form at one or several points in the research process – for example, a teacher agreeing to take part in a face-to-face interview); or passively, through opt-out procedures (such as when participants or their representatives only return the form if they decline to take part – for example, parents opting out prior to a questionnaire being distributed to all children in a school).

This process may be more challenging in research conducted in settings where it may be unusual, undesirable or unfeasible to request written confirmation of verbal agreements, such as research in different cultural contexts, research with participants whose levels of literacy may not permit signed consent, or research in virtual environments (Eynon et al., 2008). Such research may require more creative ways of documenting consent, such as the recording of verbal agreement, or using electronic markers of consent. While documenting consent is important, more important still is ensuring that consent is genuine and is monitored on an ongoing basis, rather than seen as a one-off event that subsequently may become a form of implicit constraint on the participants.

Research in schools and other educational settings comes with its own constraints around procedures for obtaining voluntary informed consent. Some of these complications arise from the asymmetrical nature of educational relationships, others from the variable ability, among potential participants, to offer informed consent. For example, will consent be entirely voluntary when given after a letter or a message from someone in position of authority, such as the school's headteacher (see Example 3.1)? Will people feel that they are free to say 'no' or to withdraw at any time with no consequences for themselves? What if a teacher researches her own practice – will her pupils be in a position to withhold their assent?

Similarly, how much age-relevant information about a project ought to be offered to potential participants, and what kinds of checks need to be in place to ensure that they understood it, in order to assert confidently that the participants have made an informed decision? Both of these issues are heightened in research that involves children. In this case, common practice is to request consent from the parents or other legal representatives on behalf of the minor; many researchers also secure the minor's assent to participate, and develop protocols for continuous monitoring of assent (particularly in the case of very young children) and plans for taking action if, at any point, that assent is withdrawn.

EXAMPLE 3.2

Food for Thought: Hypothetical Examples

A headteacher gives permission to a researcher to carry out an observational study (involving no audiovisual recording) of morning assembly in her school, as she believes that the research would benefit teachers and pupils. However, she makes the researcher aware that writing to parents is likely to elicit negative reactions. Will the headteacher's permission suffice in order to carry out the study? Read Homan (2004) for more about responsible gatekeepers and privileged access.

A researcher plans to study primary school children's use of language to construct gender. She has concerns about the validity and authenticity of the study if its aims are disclosed to the children being observed and interviewed. Therefore she decides to seek permission from the teachers and informed consent from the parents (giving both groups full information about the aims and focus of the project), while presenting the study as being about games and friendships to the children. Is her decision justified? Read Alderson and Morrow (2011: chapter 8) for more about children's assent and the limits of 'informed' consent/assent.

In planning a study set in a tightly knit community with a strong oral culture and tradition, a researcher becomes aware that seeking individual consent from members of the community once the consent of a main authority figure (gatekeeper) had been publicly granted might be seen as undermining that authority. In addition, she realizes that seeking written consent in addition to verbal consent may be seen as a signal of distrust. Should she insist on documenting written, individual consent? Read Gomm (2004) for more about ethical challenges of research in different cultural settings.

3.4.2 Trust

In their work, researchers are entrusted with information about participants, much of which is of a personal and sensitive nature. There are very clear legal contexts for the recording, storage, archiving and use of some elements of personal data, such as, in the UK, the Data Protection Act 1998. These legal requirements apply to personal data collected for research purposes, as well as to data originally collected for other purposes, but that researchers may wish to access and use in new projects. Ethical regulation, such as that of the ESRC or of the European Commission (Box 3.2), includes detailed recommendations for the recording, storage and archiving of research data in compliance with current legislation.

EXAMPLE 3.3

Challenges of Trust and Confidentiality

Three years ago, while a tenured professor on sabbatical, I conducted research by enrolling as a freshman in my own university. ...

The semester after I finished my research, I was walking out of a building just as a student from one of my freshman task groups was walking in. We exchanged warm 'how you doin'?' small talk. Then my friend asked where I was headed, and I told her that I was going to class.

'What is it?' she asked.

'Oh, an anthropology class … actually I'm teaching it.'

'No kidding!' she exclaimed. 'How did you get to do that? I want to take it!'

'Well,' I answered sheepishly, 'it's 'cause I'm actually a professor, too. I was a student last year to do some research, but now I'm back to being a professor.'

'I can't believe that,' she responded and then paused. 'I feel fooled.' (Nathan, 2005a)

See also Nathan's book, *My Freshman Year* (Nathan, 2005b).

However, the issues of privacy, anonymity and confidentiality cannot be reduced to mere compliance with predetermined sets of legal and technical requirements. Example 3.2 is based on research that had received ethical clearance, did not use any of the participants' real names and affiliations, and was originally published under a pseudonym, in an attempt to protect participants' identity. As it turned out, such measures were not enough: participants experienced psychological distress, while the cover of anonymity proved flimsy in the longer term.

Privacy refers to the individuals' right to control the disclosure of what they deem personal or non-public information about themselves. There is legal provision in many countries to protect the right to privacy (for example, legislation around the disclosure of personal data). The right to privacy may be seen as people's right to be free from any research intervention that they may construe as unwelcome and intrusive, and to withhold any information that they deem personal or sensitive. However, the boundaries around what is considered private may vary in different cultures and across time, as well as in relation to individual life histories and experience, and are particularly difficult to define in areas such as internet research (Jones, 2011) or visual research (Wiles et al., 2008).

Researchers need to be alert to the fact that invasions of privacy are possible at all stages of research, from the choice of topic to publication and beyond (for example, in storing, archiving, following-up and replicating research). The notion of secrecy, rather than privacy, is often used in relation to collective agents, such as groups, communities and organizations, particularly in situations where expectations of secrecy may clash with demands for public accountability.

Confidentiality arises from respect for the right to privacy, and functions as a 'precautionary principle' (Hammersley and Traianou, 2012: 121). Research interactions, from questionnaires to interviews and observations, are based on respondents' choice to disclose information to the researchers, some of which may be sensitive. In most cases, this disclosure happens in confidence: that is, on the basis of researchers' assurance that the connection between the individual respondent and the information disclosed will not be made known to third parties by the researcher, nor will it be able to be inferred from the research report. In order to achieve this, researchers may decide to only offer aggregate, composite (for example, 'typical' or 'average' respondents), or fictionalized accounts of the data. They will also make sure that data are stored securely and that access to them is tightly controlled, over the duration of the project and beyond.

However, maintaining confidentiality is not always straightforward. Gatekeepers and other members of a community may use a wide range of contextual clues to infer the identity of people quoted in a research report; for example, a headteacher may be able to infer the identity of individual subject teachers from her school. There may also be situations where keeping information to oneself may be too emotionally challenging for the researcher, or when the researcher may experience conflict between continuing to seek knowledge (thus maintaining secrecy) and refusing to connive with participants at what she sees as morally unacceptable behaviour. Confiding in others in such cases may lead to breaks of confidentiality. In some situations where the researcher comes across information about criminal activity or dangerous behaviour, for example, she may be legally required to disclose information to the relevant authorities.

One of the strategies used by researchers to ensure confidentiality (and protect participants from harm) is to remove any information from the data they store and analyse that may make individual respondents easily traceable and identifiable. This strategy is known as *anonymization*. Commonly used anonymization techniques include: deleting personal information (name, job title, place of work, name of school, dates and places of crucial events, detailed institutional descriptors, and other information that the researcher deems relevant), from the data or replacing it with aliases and more generic categories; using numerical identifiers; and storing any personal information completely separately from the data.

However, anonymity, in some forms of qualitative research in particular, is often a matter of degree, rather than being clear-cut (Hammersley and Traianou, 2012). For example, in some closed-question **survey** research that collects no identifying information from the respondents, anonymity (including anonymity to the researchers) can be almost complete. Meanwhile, it is very difficult, if not impossible, to guarantee it in, say, face-to-face in-depth interview research, or in visual research. In such cases, non-traceability, rather than full anonymity, may be a more realistic aim. A further complication arises in research situations where participants may actually prefer to be named in the research report, either personally or institutionally. This might be the case when they assert a level of ownership of the material they produced (for example, in some online research, or in **action research**; see Simons, 2009), or when there is a concern about possible misrepresentation of participants through anonymized, aggregated or fictionalized accounts (such as in some ethnographic research on personally, institutionally or politically sensitive issues – see Walford, 2005; Pendlebury and Enslin, 2001).

EXAMPLE 3.4

Food for Thought: Hypothetical Examples

While conducting research with children and their families, a researcher comes across evidence of violent treatment in the home and decides to break the confidentiality agreement and inform the relevant authorities. For more about whistle-blowing and disclosure, see McNamee and Bridges (2002: chapter 8) and Holmes (1998).

A study of young people's gap year experiences uses blog data. The researcher reasons that – as the blogs are publicly available – no consent procedures are required, but is concerned that some of the bloggers may have written about personal issues and given personal details while not fully aware of how public the information would be once online. She decides that blog URLs and bloggers' names should not be given in her thesis. However, she wonders whether using unattributed quotes may go against some bloggers' likely wish to be recognized for what they wrote in the blog. For more about the boundaries between public and private data online, see Snee (2010).

3.4.3   Beneficence

Research is commonly expected to minimize the risk of causing harm (*non-maleficence*), to carry out worthwhile and potentially beneficial work (*beneficence*) and to distribute any benefits and risks non-discriminatorily throughout a research project and beyond (*fairness*). (For critiques of rationalist, distributive justice models of ethical practice, see Edwards and Mauthner, 2002.) Sometimes these aims may pull in different directions, however; for example, an intervention design may at the same time withhold or delay potential benefits from a control group, and/or expose the intervention group to unknown risks. Balancing these risks may involve a detailed risk assessment, coupled with identifying an alternative set of benefits to be offered to the control group.

There are many different types of *harm* (or damage) that may be associated with research, such as, at the individual level, physical, psychological, social and reputational, and practical and occupational harm (Hammersley and Traianou, 2012). Those exposed to the risk of harm may be individual participants, their peers, families or acquaintances, but also individual researchers and members of their networks. Organizations, communities and professions may also be at risk: for example, research and the publication of its outcomes may pose economic threats to an organization, or bring a professional group into disrepute. The threshold for what counts as more or less severe and long-lasting harm, thus for the perceived acceptability of different research practices, may vary, historically, culturally and contextually. In addition, not all harms connected to research may be the full responsibility of the researcher; for example, damage may arise from subsequent, hard-to-anticipate uses of research. Assessing and monitoring risks, seeing consent and confidentiality as ongoing rather than one-off events, and taking relevant insurance may help minimize the risk of harm and contain its impact. However, none of these strategies is foolproof; it is not feasible to anticipate and deflect all potential risks, and there may be differences of opinion about the likelihood and seriousness of particular risks among those involved in a project (Example 3.3).

EXAMPLE 3.5

Challenges in Anticipating Harms

The primary purpose of the ethics procedure that we were subject to is stated to be the protection of potential research participants (and researchers). In our case those participants were specific teachers who had been accused of sexual abuse, members of their families, their colleagues, and people associated with their schools. However, we were being taken to task for failing to protect unknown and, most significantly, hypothetical children who were to play no part in the research process. While we appreciate and accept the need to attempt to anticipate unforeseen consequences arising in the course of, or subsequently to, an actual project, we feel that it is quite another matter to have to try to predict future damage to people who are entirely unconnected to and uninvolved in, that research. Such forecasting and pre-empting of problems is, we would suggest, beyond the scope of most mortals. Also, seeking to obviate all possible risk could lead to a situation where only the most anodyne of projects would receive clearance. (Sikes and Piper, 2010: 29–30)

The concept of *benefits* is also complex and situated. Research takes time and effort, and some of that time and effort belongs to the participants, whether they are children and young people, teachers and headteachers, administrators or policy-makers. Does the expected outcome of research, in both terms of advancement and corroboration of knowledge and of practical collective or individual benefit, justify the burden placed on participants?

Arguably, the most important benefit of research is the creation of valuable knowledge (Hammersley and Traianou, 2012). As Denzin (1997) argued in relation to ethnography, the act of writing itself, and the sharing of the writing with others, can be powerful acts of moral discovery and social and political transformation. Further potential benefits include: learning and educational outcomes and support; therapeutic effects of research; enjoyment and sense of belonging and empowerment; relationships and networking; or services provided by researchers in the setting, for example, in some forms of participatory research (language teaching, extracurricular activities, writing and filing documents, driving). Common practices aimed at protecting children and other vulnerable groups are to avoid offering any financial incentives for participation in research (reimbursement of travel expenses does not fall into this category) and to scrutinize carefully the use of any other inducements to recruit and retain participants. Some forms of post-participation *reward*, such as book tokens or participation in educationally worthwhile activities, may be deemed acceptable, depending on circumstances. Certificates of participation in research or stickers (in the case of children), thank you letters or cards, or, as appropriate in light of confidentiality agreements, acknowledgement in publications may also be acceptable forms of non-financial recognition. In research with children, regardless of potential benefits, there is an expectation that risk and burden would both be minimal, in relation to an ideal 'no harm' situation.

The positioning of the researcher within, or relative to, the field of her research is also important. For example, how do researchers' personal values affect their approach to the research, their interpretations, and their judgements about ethical courses of action? Further, is it ethical to research a community with which you cannot empathize? (Figueroa, in Simmons and Usher, 2000: 88). Personal values and lack of empathy may make it difficult for researchers to avoid silencing or marginalizing particular concerns of the participants (McNamee and Bridges, 2002). Reflexivity in analysis and writing and participant involvement may help alleviate some of these issues.

Depending on the approach taken to research, participants can be engaged in checking interpretations of the data, in seeking alternative interpretations, and in exploring their implications. Sometimes, such as in the case of research conducted with vulnerable participants or in disadvantaged communities, it can be very tempting to extend the role of the researcher into political activism, advocacy and support; in other words, to prioritize reciprocity and voice over the articulation and communication of knowledge. This can be a very fulfilling personal project for the researcher, but may make it more difficult to produce and publish a report from the work – hence, to gain a PhD, in the case of doctoral research – and to disengage from the field after the end of a project. The question is how to maintain a balance between rigour in research and care for the participants and their setting.

—————————————————————— **EXAMPLE 3.6** ——————————————————————

Food for Thought: Hypothetical Examples

A researcher is working with adolescent girls who have been victims of abuse. She is committed to telling participants' stories in an authentic, credible and convincing way. She sees her role as enabling the voices of these young women to be heard in professional arenas. Her participants see her as empathetic and trustworthy and speak openly to her; the interviews have a thera-peutic tone. However, despite her best intentions, after the publication of the report some of the participants feel exposed and experience psychological distress, a sense of betrayal, hurt, and outrage. For more about activism and voice, see Thomson (2008).

An intervention study uses random allocation of 7-year-olds from one school to experimental and control groups. The experimental group receives 6 months of intensive supplementary support for reading, delivered by a trained assistant and using an electronic platform, while the control group continues as before, with no supplementary support. The researchers see this design as a highly efficient way of generating good data, but are concerned about issues of fairness involved in withholding support from the control group for the duration of the intervention. For more about benefits to participants, see Eynon et al. (2008).

A researcher uses photographs taken by children in their community. Children and parents have consented to participation in the project and have assigned copyright over the images to the researchers, on the formal understanding that all the faces in the photographs will have been blurred prior to being stored on the researchers' computer. The researchers wish to use the images in the following contexts: (a) in a presentation about research, with no handouts; (b) in the published report; (c) as part of a qualitative data archive, for other researchers to use. They feel that each of these contexts raises distinctive ethical issues and end up using the images on the basis of the original consent in (a), seeking further, image-by-image, consent for (b), and decid-ing against (c). For more about ethical responsibilities in visual research, see Wiles et al. (2008).

———

3.5 THE ETHICS OF STUDENT RESEARCH AS SITUATED DELIBERATION

Ethical codes vary in structure and content. For example, they may engage more or less explicitly with the moral underpinnings of procedural requirements. In terms of content, they may vary in how they balance generic rules for academic conduct with principles and rules guiding the relationship between researchers or research institu-tions and participants and beneficiaries. No code is perfect, and no attempt to apply it to real-life research situations is entirely straightforward.

Therefore, codes leave important spaces for institutions, teams and individual researchers to deliberate about what would be an ethically acceptable course of action in particular research situations and contexts. The link between abstract and general principles and standards and concrete and particular situations is the responsibility of the researchers, who interpret them in the light of values specific to research as a form of practice focused on generating knowledge (Pring, 2004). Hammersley and Traianou (2012: 36) see research ethics as 'a form of occupational ethics: it is about what social researchers ought, and ought not, to do *as researchers*, and/or about what count as vices and virtues *in doing research*'.

As explained in this chapter, thinking about ethics in research involves constant questioning of both the aims and means of research, drawing on first-hand under-standing of the particular actors and circumstances of a research situation as it unfolds. Justifying ethical decisions is a matter of principled reasoning as well as of active commitment – an ongoing process throughout which researchers need to pay atten-tion to the situation and the ways in which it shapes their judgement. To paraphrase McNamee (McNamee and Bridges, 2002: 13), it is *this* particular researcher (or team) in *this* particular set of circumstances who needs to exercise context-sensitive judgement and embed it in her practice. That is to say, the researcher must identify the ethically salient aspects of a situation and connect them, as appropriate, with principles, rules, outcomes, and other cases, in order to act ethically throughout the life span of a research project.

The relationships between the researcher herself (or himself), and others (including relevant communities of research practice) are at the centre of situated ethical delibera-tion. A researcher may enter a research situation with a range of roles and aims that may be in conflict with each other and which, therefore, need to be negotiated in her research practice. This practice may be subject to many, sometimes contradictory, demands. Figure 3.1 illustrates some of the different demands placed upon research, the criteria of acceptability shaping it, and the ethical traditions framing it. To start with, research is subject to legal requirements; it is guided by ethical codes, institutional pro-cedures (such as ethical clearance requirements in universities), and methodological and technical requirements; in the case of student research, it is shaped by course require-ments, including definitions of success and assessment criteria. As a form of practice, it is also expected to articulate with other practices, including teaching, learning, and policy-making. Further, by virtue of its being research, rather than any other form of professional practice, it has epistemic aims and draws on methodological and substan-tive theories and philosophical approaches. These demands form a space of values that is specific to research, as distinct from other practices. Research that negotiates these different positions and demands successfully while maintaining integrity is deemed 'acceptable' in a range of ways – procedurally, technically, epistemologically, morally, and socio-culturally.

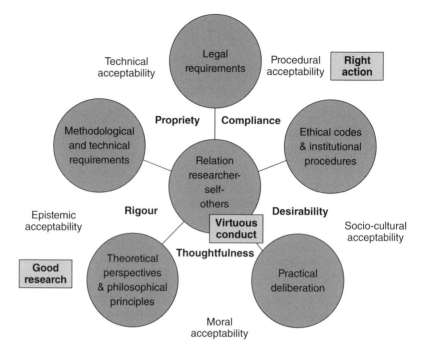

Figure 3.1 Research ethics as situated deliberation

The complexity of the contexts and demands illustrated in Figure 3.1 and of the judgements, including moral, required to navigate them suggests that research ethics is more than the linear application of specific rules to get out of dilemmas and to comply with institutional requirements. It involves reflective deliberation that draws on rich understanding of concrete situations and can employ ways of reasoning and doing that may be associated with more than one tradition of ethics. It can also be experienced as an emotionally charged process, fraught with indecision, frustration, or, sometimes, a sense of guilt. As research ethics concerns not only the treatment of others (from participants and gatekeepers to peers), but also the self, the ways in which researchers recognize and make sense of these emotions are part of the overall ethical texture of a research project.

3.6 SUMMARY

Ethical action in research arises from rich, context-sensitive deliberation at the intersection of practical wisdom, theoretical understanding and principled reasoning.

Different traditions in philosophical ethics, including duty, consequence, virtue and situated ethics, may help researchers identify the ethically salient aspects of a research situation, reflect on the relative worth of different courses of action available to them, and act ethically throughout the research process

Ethical codes and guidelines may offer further resources for ethical deliberation, as well as providing the procedural framework for institutional sanctioning of researchers' chosen courses of action and actual conduct.

For individual researchers, it is important not just to achieve technical compliance (thus ethical 'approval' or 'clearance') of their projects with ethical codes and other procedural requirements, as stipulated in checklists, guidebooks and forms, but also to develop their personal understanding of ethical principles and contexts, their commitment to ethical research, and the ability to act wisely in ethically complex situations.

3.7 REVIEW CONCEPTS

Ethics   The study of what are good, right or virtuous courses of action; can be approached from different points of view.

Deontological ethics   Emphasizes acting out of duty, as opposed to pleasure, inclination or interest. What is the right course of action in this situation?

Teleological ethics   Emphasizes choosing the best course of action, using the 'greatest happiness' or 'utility' principle. What course of action in this situation is likely to result in the greatest good for all concerned?

Aretaic ethics   Emphasizes the most virtuous ways of being and living. What course of action in this situation accords with the traits or dispositions of the virtuous person?

Situational ethics   Emphasizes that ethical decisions are contextual, and are never neatly defined or fully resolved.

Ethical codes   Negotiated agreements from professional associations about acceptable practice in particular professional, occupational and institutional contexts; tend to include detailed rules for conducting research.

Principle of autonomy   The obligation on the part of the investigator to respect each participant as a person capable of making an informed decision regarding participation in the research study.

Principle of trust   The obligation of investigators to safeguard the information entrusted to them by participants in the research; includes the principles of confidentiality, privacy and anonymity.

Principle of beneficence   The obligation on the part of the investigator to attempt to maximize benefits for the individual participant and/or society, while minimizing risk of harm to the individual.

Research ethics as situated deliberation   Researchers need to interpret ethical codes – which often include abstract principles and standards – in the context of particular research situations.

———————— **EXERCISES AND STUDY QUESTIONS** ————————

1. Describe what is meant by each of these:

   - Deontological approach to ethical issues
   - Teleological approach to ethical issues
   - Aretaic approach to ethical issues
   - Situational approach to ethical issues

2. Apply each of these four approaches to the hypothetical examples in Examples 3.2, 3.4 and 3.6. What conclusions do the different approaches lead to for each of the situations?
3. What similarities do you see in these four approaches? What differences do you see?
4. Study one of the codes of ethics for education research referred to in Box 1.2. How helpful would this code be in helping with ethical issues in your proposed research? What difficulties would it lead to?
5. Read through the codes of ethics for research in another area of social science – for example, the British Sociological Association (http://www.britsoc.co.uk/media/27107/StatementofEthicalPractice.pdf), or the American Psychological Association (http://www.apa.org/ethics/code/index.aspx). To what extent do you think they are helpful? What difficulties do you think they might lead to? Does anything you read in them surprise you?

4

DEVELOPING A GENERAL FRAMEWORK FOR PROPOSALS

This chapter describes a general framework for developing and organizing research proposals, focusing on the central role of research questions. While this description has organization and structure, this does not mean that developing a proposal does (or should) proceed in the tidy, organized, deductive way that might be inferred from this description. It is possible for a proposal to develop in this way. But it is more likely that its development will be a messy, cyclical process, with hesitations and frustrations, where the researcher cycles backwards and forwards between different issues and different sections, iterating towards a final version. This echoes the process–product distinction noted in Chapter 2. The process is untidy, but the product is (expected to be) neat, well structured and easy to follow.

4.1 AN OVERALL FRAMEWORK

Chapter 2 suggested that the proposal must deal with these main themes:

- what the proposed research is about;
- what it is trying to find out or achieve;
- how it will go about doing that;
- what we will learn from that and why it is worth learning.

We can now represent these themes in three general but central questions, which the proposal needs to answer:

- What?
- How?
- Why?

These three general questions are at the heart of the proposal. Together they form an overall framework for its development:

- *What* means what this research is trying to find out (or do, or achieve). Phrased this way, it points directly to research questions.
- *How* means how the research proposes to answer its questions. Answering the 'how' question means describing the methods of the research. Methods are seen here as dependent on research questions.
- *Why* means why this research is worth doing. This points to the justification (or significance, or importance, or contribution, or expected outcomes) of the research. It acknowledges that all research requires the investment of considerable time, energy and other resources, and it asks for justification of that investment. It also involves the idea of the proposal (and research) as a coherent argument. To some extent, the argument presented in the proposal should itself answer the question of why the research is worth doing. In addition, as suggested in Chapter 7, there is usually another section in the proposal which addresses explicitly the justification or contribution of the proposed research.

Generally speaking, a good way to proceed in developing a proposal is to work on 'what' before 'how' (see Section 4.7.2). Therefore, this chapter concentrates on research questions. Putting the 'what' before the 'how' means putting questions before methods. Methods are dealt with in Chapter 6.

4.2 A HIERARCHY OF CONCEPTS

One advantage of planning research in terms of research questions is that it makes explicit the idea of levels of abstraction in research. We can distinguish five levels of concepts and questions, which vary in levels of abstraction, forming an inductive–deductive **hierarchy**:

- research area;
- research topic;
- general research questions;
- specific research questions;
- **data collection questions**.

To say that these five things form a hierarchy is to say that they vary systematically in levels of abstraction and generality, and that they need to be connected to each other logically, by **induction** and **deduction**, across those levels. The top level is the most general and the most abstract. The bottom level is the most specific and the most concrete.

Thus, from the top down, the research area is more general than the research topic, which itself is more general than the general research question(s), which are more general than the specific research questions, which in turn are more general than the data collection questions.

Another way of saying this, and now moving from the bottom up, is that the data collection questions follow on from (or are implied by, or are included in), the specific research questions, which in turn follow on from (or are implied by or are included in) the general research questions, and so on up the hierarchy.

A benefit of thinking this way, and of organizing research this way, is that it exposes and highlights the links between these different levels of abstraction. It is necessary to have tight logical links between these levels for the research to have **internal** consistency, coherence and **validity**. This is what is meant by 'follow on from' in the paragraph above. The technical concepts or processes involved here are deduction and induction. We move downwards in the hierarchy by deduction, and upwards by induction. Both processes are governed by logic.

Not all research projects can be organized or planned this way. In particular, those which have a more unfolding design would not fit easily with this highly prestructured approach. There are also issues about 'generalizing' versus 'particularizing' research questions

(Maxwell, 2012),[1] and the intended emphasis on one of these types of question or the other in a particular study. At the same time, however, many projects do fit well into this approach, and, in any case, this hierarchy of concepts is useful both pedagogically and practically. Not only does thinking in these terms help to organize the developing proposal; but it also helps you to communicate clearly about your research, and to write the proposal (and, later on, the dissertation). And if a study emphasizes particularizing question(s), working through these levels of abstraction helps to sharpen its logic and to strengthen its internal validity.

4.3 RESEARCH AREAS AND TOPICS

Research areas are usually stated in a few words, and sometimes just one word. Topics similarly are a few words, but usually more than those describing the research area. The topic falls within the area. It is an aspect, or a part, of the area – a step towards making the general area more specific. It is included in the area, but it is, of course, not the only topic within the area.

Table 4.1 From research area to research topics

Research area

Youth suicide

Four possible research topics

1   Suicide rates among different groups
2   Factors associated with the incidence of youth suicide
3   Managing suicide behaviour among teenagers
4   Youth culture and the meaning of suicide

Note

Topics 1 and 2 imply a predominantly quantitative approach.

Topics 3 and 4 imply a predominantly qualitative approach.

Examples of research areas are absenteeism at work, youth subculture in high schools, living with Tourette's syndrome, academic success and failure at university, membership of voluntary organizations, and youth suicide. Four possible research topics within the research area of youth suicide are shown in Table 4.1.

Identifying first the research area, and then the topic within the area, immediately gives a first level of focus to the research, a first narrowing of the possibilities.

---

[1]A generalizing question seeks nomothetic knowledge – universalized law-like statements applying generally across a class of people, situations, events or phenomena. A particularizing question seeks ideographic knowledge – local, case-based, specific propositions.

Of course, any research area includes many topics, so two decisions are involved here: the first is the selection of an area, the second is the selection of a topic within the area. Students may not have so much difficulty with the first decision, the area. They know generally what research area they are interested in. They often have rather more difficulty with the second decision: with all these possible topics within this area, which should I choose?

A valuable consequence of identifying the research area is that it enables you as the researcher immediately to connect your work to the literature. It defines a body of literature as relevant to this piece of research. Identifying a topic within an area gives still more specific direction to the literature. It enables a more specific body of literature to be identified as centrally relevant to the research.

4.4   GENERAL AND SPECIFIC RESEARCH QUESTIONS

General and specific research questions bring things down to the next level of specificity, further narrowing the focus of the proposed research. The distinction between them is in terms of specificity. General research questions are more abstract and (usually) not directly answerable. Specific research questions are more detailed and concrete; they are directly answerable because they point directly at the data needed to answer them. This point is elaborated in Section 4.6.

Just as there are many research topics within a research area, so there are many possible general research questions within a research topic. As indicated in Section 2.6, a convincing way of connecting topic to general research questions is through problem and purpose – to identify the problem behind the research, and to state the general purpose as a way of dealing with or solving the problem. This general purpose statement can then be translated into general research questions. Specific research questions take the deductive process further, subdividing a general question into the specific questions which follow from it.

Table 4.2   From research topic to general research questions

---

Research topic

Factors associated with the incidence of youth suicide

General research question 1

What is the relationship between family background factors and the incidence of youth suicide?

General research question 2

What is the relationship between school experience factors and the incidence of youth suicide?

Note

More general research questions are possible. These are only two examples. As noted in Table 4.1, this topic and these general questions, as phrased, have a quantitative bias.

Table 4.3 From general research question to specific research questions

---

General research question

What is the relationship between family background factors and the incidence of youth suicide?

Specific research question 1

What is the relationship between family income and the incidence of youth suicide?

or

Do youth suicide rates differ between families of different income levels?

Specific research question 2

What is the relationship between parental break-up and the incidence of youth suicide?

or

Do youth suicide rates differ between families where parents are divorced or separated, and families where they are not?

Note

More specific research questions are possible. These are only two examples.

A general question is normally too broad to be answered directly, too broad to satisfy the empirical criterion (see Section 4.6). Its concepts are too general. It therefore requires logical subdivision into several specific research questions. The general research question is answered indirectly by accumulating and integrating the answers to the corresponding specific research questions. A study may well have more than one general research question. In that case, each will require analysis and subdivision into appropriate specific research questions. Tables 4.2 and 4.3 illustrate this process with the research area of youth suicide.

This distinction is really a matter of common sense, and, in the practical business of planning research, is not difficult to make. And, as already noted, while the description here is presented deductively, it is by no means necessary for things to proceed that way. They may also proceed inductively, and, as is probably most common, by some cyclical and iterative mixture of induction and deduction.

In formal terms, a good way to distinguish general from specific research questions is to apply the empirical criterion (Section 4.6) to each question, as it is developed: is it clear what data will be required to answer this question? If the answer for each question is yes, we can proceed from questions to methods. If the answer is no, one thing probably needed is further specificity. This criterion is also a good check on deciding whether we have reached a set of researchable questions.

At the heart of this discussion is the process of making a general concept more specific by showing its dimensions, aspects, factors, components or indicators. In effect, you are defining a general concept 'downwards' towards its data indicators. Of the several terms given above (dimensions, aspects, factors, components, indicators), I prefer the term *indicators* because of its wide applicability across different types of research. It applies in quantitative and qualitative contexts, whereas the terms 'dimensions', 'factors' and 'components' have more quantitative connotations.

A proviso, more likely to be needed in qualitative studies, is that the research may proceed upwards in abstraction from indicators to general concepts, rather than downwards in abstraction from general concepts to indicators. To repeat, the important thing is not which way the research proceeds. You can proceed downwards, using deduction, from general concept to specific concept to indicators, or you can proceed upwards, using induction, from indicators to specific and general concepts. Or you can use both deduction and induction. The important thing is that the finished product as a proposal (and, ultimately, as a piece of research) shows logical connections across the different levels of abstraction.

4.5 DATA COLLECTION QUESTIONS

At the lowest level in this hierarchy come data collection questions. They are questions at the most specific level.

The reason for separating out data collection questions here is that students sometimes confuse research questions with data collection questions. A research question is a question the research itself is trying to answer. A data collection question is a question which is asked in order to collect data in order to help answer the research question. In that sense, it is more specific still than the research question. In that sense too, more than one data collection question, sometimes several and sometimes many, will be involved in assembling the data necessary to answer one research question.[2]

What does this hierarchy of concepts mean for proposal development? I have gone into this detailed analysis because it is often a central aspect of the pre-empirical, setting-up stage of the research, and because it shows clearly the differing levels of abstraction. Understanding this hierarchy of concepts is important, but it is unlikely to be applicable, formula-like, in proposal development. As already noted, the question

---

[2]This does not apply literally to all actual data collection questions which might be used in a study. Thus some data collection questions might themselves be quite general questions – for example, introductory or 'grand tour' questions in a qualitative research interview. But the point being made here is that the role of most data collection questions in the research is to operate at the most specific level. As Maxwell (2012) says, research questions identify what you want to understand; interview questions, which are data collection questions, provide the data you need to understand these things. The same is true of survey questions. Being the most specific level of questions, the actual data collection questions will probably not be shown in the proposal.

development stage is likely to be messy, iterative and cyclical, and it can proceed any way at all.[3] But if you are aware of this hierarchy, you can use it to help disentangle and organize the many questions which serious consideration of almost any research area and topic will produce.

4.6 RESEARCH QUESTIONS AND DATA: THE EMPIRICAL CRITERION

In empirical research, it is necessary that data be linked to concepts, and concepts to data, and the links between concepts and data must be tight, logical and consistent. This idea needs to be applied to our research questions.

Concepts are embedded in research questions. General questions use general concepts, and specific questions use specific concepts. General concepts are typically too abstract to be linked directly to data indicators. Rather, they are linked indirectly to data through specific concepts. Translating general concepts down to specific concepts means specifying what the researcher will take to be indicators, in the empirical data, of these concepts.

The idea of the empirical criterion for research questions is that a well-developed and well-stated research question indicates what data will be necessary to answer it. It is the idea behind the expression that: 'a question well asked is a question half answered'. Ultimately, each research question needs to be phrased at such a level of specificity that we can see what data we will require in order to answer it.

We can routinely apply this empirical criterion to research questions as they are developed. For each question, is it clear what data will be required to answer the question? If the research questions do not give clear indications of the data needed to answer them, we will not know how to proceed in the research when it comes to the data collection and analysis stages.

One common example of this concerns 'should' questions, which arise frequently when students are first planning research. It is worth looking at this in some detail, both because it illustrates the point being made in this section, and because it arises frequently. By 'should' questions, I mean such questions as:

- Should teachers assess students? Should teachers know the IQ of students? Should teachers use corporal punishment?

---

[3]Locke et al. (2011) give examples of this question development process, including inductively and deductively. Maxwell (2012), writing for qualitative research, makes distinctions between research questions (generalizing–particularizing, instrumentalist–realist, variance–process). He also gives an example of the development of research questions, and gives an exercise to assist in this. Madsen (1983: 30–4) shows how to develop subsidiary (that is, specific) research questions from a general question.

- Should nurses wear white uniforms? Should nurses allow patients to participate in care planning (Brink and Wood, 1994: 8)?
- Should managers use democratic or authoritarian leadership styles? Should organizations have a flat structure or a hierarchical structure?

Such questions are complex, not least because they involve (or appear to involve) a **value judgement**. But, for our purposes in this section, these questions fail the test of the empirical criterion. Thus, for any of these 'should' questions, it is not clear what data would be required to answer them. Therefore, they are not researchable or answerable with data, as stated. They are not empirical questions, as they stand, and they need rephrasing if they are to be answered by empirical research.

I am not saying that these value questions are unimportant questions. On the contrary, a strong argument can be made that 'should' questions are among the most important types of questions that we need to answer. I am only saying that they are not empirical questions, as phrased, and therefore they need either to be answered using methods which are not empirical, or to be rephrased to make them empirical.

Usually such questions can be rephrased, to make them answerable empirically. There are different ways this can be done. One simple way, which is often helpful, is to rephrase using 'Does X think that ...' (where X needs to be defined). Thus 'Should nurses wear white uniforms?' might become:

- Do nurses think they should wear white uniforms?

or

- Do hospital administrators think nurses should wear white uniforms?

or

- Do patients think nurses should wear white uniforms?

These rephrased questions now start to meet the empirical criterion. Thus, the first rephrasing clearly indicates that we will need data from nurses about their views on the wearing of white uniforms.[4] The second shows we will need similar data from hospital administrators, and so on.

---

[4]The rephrasing needs to go further than just this, for the question to meet the empirical criterion completely. Also, of course, there are other ways of rephrasing the original 'should' question. This simple way has been used for illustration, but this way of rephrasing might well be part of any evaluative answer to the original question, even though it changes its meaning somewhat. Another way is to rephrase the 'should' question in terms of means and ends (or causes and effects). For example, 'Should nurses wear white uniforms?' might become 'What consequences does the wearing of white uniforms have on nurse–doctor–patient relationships, or on patients' attitudes?'

To sum up, as you develop your research questions, you should ask, for each question, 'What data are needed to answer this question?'

4.7 THREE TACTICAL ISSUES

Chapter 8 deals with some general and specific tactics in developing a proposal. In addition to that discussion, three tactical issues are noted here, because they fit in well with the content of this chapter. They are:

- the importance of the pre-empirical stage of research;
- questions before methods;
- whether you need hypotheses.

4.7.1 The importance of the pre-empirical stage

The pre-empirical stage of research refers to the issues discussed in this chapter, and also in Chapter 5. I use the term 'question development' to describe this stage of the analysis and development of the research questions. In my opinion, it is just as important as the empirical or methods stage of the research. It is really where things are set up, and it therefore has an important determining influence on what is done later – although, naturally, that influence is more important in prestructured than in unfolding studies. But its importance is not very often stressed in the research methods literature. I think that has been partly because of the preoccupation in the field with methodological issues. I do not say that these methodological issues are unimportant. Rather, I want to counterbalance them by stressing the importance of the question development and conceptual analysis work required in the pre-empirical stage. A crucial step in this pre-empirical work is the selection and identification of research area and topic. Once these decisions are clear in the research student's mind, a great deal has been achieved.

4.7.2 Questions before methods

Questions and methods need to be aligned with each other in a piece of research. This is part of the internal validity of a piece of research, and is more important than ever in social science research today, where quantitative and qualitative methods sit alongside each other and may be combined in the one study.

In general, the best way to achieve this alignment is to focus first on developing the research questions, and second on methods to answer those questions. 'In general' in this sentence means that there are exceptions to this order of events, and that it is not mandatory. But I recommend it because I have found that it is common that research students worry about issues of method in advance of getting a clear view of the research questions. Too often, a student wants to ask, too early, 'How will I do this?' or 'Can I use such and such a method?' Those questions of course have their place. But that place is not so early in the process of planning the research that they come before the substantive issues dealing with what the research is trying to find out.

4.7.3 Do I need hypotheses in my proposal?

On a much more specific level, I single out the question 'Do I need hypotheses?' because I find it comes up frequently and causes confusion. I believe that hypotheses should be used in research as and when appropriate, rather than in some mandatory or automatic way. This belief is based on the view that hypotheses have an important function in research when they can be deduced from a theory, or when they are explained by a theory, so that the research, in testing the hypotheses, is really testing the theory behind the hypotheses.

This is the 'classical' or traditional **hypothetico-deductive** model of research, and it has its place and its importance. But not all social research does or should align itself with this model. There are two straightforward questions which can help in determining whether hypotheses are appropriate in a particular study:

- For each specific research question, can I predict (in advance of the empirical research – that is, in advance of getting and analysing the data) what I am likely to find?
- If so, is the basis for that prediction a rationale, some set of propositions, a 'theory' from which the hypotheses follow, and which 'explains' the hypotheses?

If the answer to these two questions is 'yes', I should by all means formulate and test hypotheses in the research, and, in so doing, test the theory. If not, I suggest we leave the matter at the level of research questions. I can see no logical difference between answering research questions and testing hypotheses, when it comes to what data we will get and how we will analyse them. The same operations are required.

This question (hypotheses or no hypotheses?) does not have to be a strict either–or matter. The idea of the 'guiding hypothesis' is often useful in research. This may be an informed guess or hunch, for which the researcher does not yet have a fully developed rationale as described above. As well as bringing together, summarizing and integrating the researcher's thinking on the topic, which is valuable, such a guiding hypothesis can also give structure to the design, data collection and data analysis aspects of the study, and can expose other concepts in the researcher's thinking. In that sense, it is useful. But research questions can fulfil these functions as well. In particular, the sometimes noted 'focusing' function of a hypothesis is just as well fulfilled by a research question.

In short, I am against the idea that we should have hypotheses in research proposals *just for the sake of having hypotheses*. Let us use them if appropriate, and not use them if not appropriate. Figure 2.1 showed a model of research built around research questions. This same model can be expanded for research which sets out to test hypotheses. The expanded model is shown in Figure 4.1.

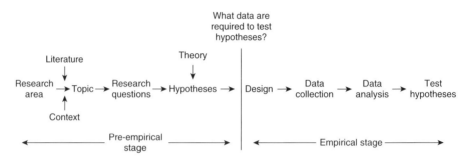

Figure 4.1 Simplified model of research (with hypotheses)

4.8 REVIEW CONCEPTS

Research area A small number of words – perhaps only one word – describing the general area of the research.

Research topic A more specific description of the particular topic the research will focus on; topics lie within areas.

General research question(s) One or more questions within the research topic that the research sets out to answer; usually too general to be directly answered, and need specification.

Specific research question(s) Derived from general research questions, more specific questions which identify the specific dimensions or aspects included in general research questions.

Data collection questions The very specific questions which together provide the data to answer the research questions; most commonly interview questions in qualitative research, and closed-ended survey questions in quantitative research.

Empirical criterion (for research questions) Summed up by the question 'Is it clear what data are needed to answer this research question?'

Hypotheses Predicted answers to research questions; in the classical hypothetico-deductive model of scientific research, hypotheses are deduced from a theory, which explains them.

──────── **EXERCISES AND STUDY QUESTIONS** ────────

1. The 'two-pager':

   In *no more than two pages*, write the following:

   (a) Questions: What are the area and topic for my research? What are the general and specific questions my research will try to answer?
   (b) Methods: In general terms, how will I go about this? Specifically, what strategy will I use (see Section 6.3), and will my research be qualitative, quantitative or mixed methods?

   Note:

   - Both (a) and (b) should be preceded by 'as best I can see things at the moment'.
   - This document gets the iterative and cumulative process of proposal development started.
   - This exercise deliberately ignores – for the moment – background, context and literature. They come in later.

2. Developing a proposal by 'working upwards'. Think of a possible research question you might be interested in, and write it down.

Now ask: At what level of abstraction is this question: is it general or specific? (Hint: is it clear what data we will need to answer it? If so it is a specific research question. If not, it is a general research question). If it is specific, what more general question does it flow from? This will give you a general research question.

Now, what topic does this general question follow from, or fit within? And taking it further, what problem (or unknown, or issue) does it proceed from?

Now see if you can fashion this into a problem–purpose statement connected by 'therefore' (for example, the problem is ... therefore the purpose of the research is ...). Think of the purpose statement as a general, overall description of what the study will try to do or find out. It may be stated as a question (for example, what is the relationship between X and Y?) or as a statement (for example, to investigate the relationship between X and Y).

3. Developing a research proposal by 'working downwards'. For this exercise, use the material on youth suicide in Chapter as a guide. Begin by rereading this chapter, especially Sections 4.3 and 4.4.

Think of an overall research area you are interested in.

Within that, identify one or more topics.

Now select one of these topics, and generate some possible research questions about this topic.

Develop each research question to the point where it is clear what data will be required to answer it.

Now go back over what you've done: identify the problem (or unknown, or issue) behind the questions you have developed and develop an overall purpose statement to show how the study will try to solve the problem. Can they be connected with 'therefore'?

Show how that overall purpose statement (or question) leads to the specific questions you have developed.

4. Whichever way you are working, as you develop your research proposal, ask yourself these questions:

- What

  - What is my research about?
  - What is its purpose?
  - What is it trying to find out or achieve?
  - Especially: What questions is it trying to answer?

- How

  - How will my research answer its questions?

- Why

  - Why is this research worth doing?

Then, at a more specific level, ask these questions:

- What is my research area? Have I clearly identified it?
- What is my topic? Have I clearly identified it and shown how it fits within the research area?
- What are my general research questions?
- What are my specific research questions?
- Does each specific research question meet the empirical criterion? Is it clear what data are required to answer each question?

5

USING THEORY AND DEALING WITH THE LITERATURE

The previous chapter dealt with an overall framework for developing proposals, and, as a practical and pedagogical device, focused on the central role of research questions. In this chapter, I look at two important and complementary issues. The first concerns theory, both methodological and substantive. The second, focusing on the literature, is concerned both with the context of the research and with the way its research questions and strategy are developed.

These issues have particular prominence here because we are looking at quantitative and qualitative research together, and we are using the same general framework of research questions, design, data collection and data analysis to do that. They also come into focus because we are looking across social science research in general, including different areas and different research styles and traditions, as well as the two main different approaches. But the issues apply unevenly and in different ways across that range. Therefore not all will need explicit treatment in all proposals. Despite that, I think they are issues that should be routinely thought about in planning research. Doing so will expose hidden assumptions, strengthen the proposal, and prepare the researcher better, especially if defence of the proposal (or, ultimately, of the dissertation) is involved.

In planning research and developing proposals, I think of these as issues that occur around and alongside the central 'what', 'how' and 'why' questions of the previous chapter. In that sense, they give context and direction to the proposed research. In some respects, too, they may change the way the 'what' questions are asked and dealt with.

The main point I want to stress with respect to both theory and literature is that the proposal writer needs to put the reader in the picture as to which of the points noted here apply in the proposed research, and in what way. That means, of course, that the writer has to work out in the planning stage of the research which of these points apply, and in what way. Doing this and communicating this is an important clarifying task for the researcher, and an important safeguard against mistaken expectations on the part of the reader.

5.1 THEORY

The term 'theory' is used in many different ways in the literature, which can create difficulties. Here, I focus on two main types of theory – methodological theory and substantive theory. Both are important. Methodological theory concerns the philosophy behind research methods, and is discussed in Section 5.2. Substantive theory concerns the content area of research, and is discussed in Section 5.4. It leads on to the topics of description and explanation (Section 5.4.1), and to theory verification and theory generation (Section 5.4.2).

5.2 METHODOLOGICAL THEORY

Methodological theory is theory about method – about what lies behind the approaches and methods of inquiry used in a piece of research. By contrast, substantive theory, to which we will turn in Section 5.4, is about substance or content in research.

Methods of inquiry are necessarily based on assumptions – assumptions about the nature of the reality being studied, assumptions about what constitutes knowledge of this reality, and assumptions about what therefore are appropriate methods for building knowledge of this reality. Very often these assumptions are implicit. A point of contention in research methods training has often been whether or not it should be required that such assumptions are made explicit in a piece of postgraduate research.

These assumptions constitute the essential idea of what is meant by the term 'paradigm' in the research methodology and philosophy of science literature. Paradigm issues are necessarily philosophical in nature. *Paradigm* means a set of assumptions about the world, and about what constitute proper topics and techniques for inquiring into that world. Put simply, it is a way of looking at the world. It entails a view of how inquiry should be done (hence the term 'inquiry paradigm' which is sometimes used), and is a broad term encompassing elements of epistemology, theory and philosophy, along with methods. Denzin and Lincoln (2013) describe a paradigm as:

> a set of basic beliefs (or metaphysics) that deals with ultimates or first principles. It represents a worldview that defines, for its holder, the nature of 'the world,' the individual's place in it, and the range of possible relationships to that world and its parts.

They point out that inquiry paradigms define what they are concerned with, and what falls within and outside the limits of legitimate inquiry, and that inquiry paradigms address three fundamental questions, which reflect the assumptions noted above:

1. The ontological question: What is the form and nature of reality and, therefore, what is there that can be known about it?
2. The epistemological question: What is the relationship between the knower and what can be known?
3. The methodological question: How can the inquirer go about finding out what can be known?

In simpler language, paradigms tell us:

- what the reality is like (ontology);
- what the relationship is between the researcher and that reality (epistemology); and
- what methods can be used for studying the reality (methodology).

These three interrelated questions illustrate the connections between methods and the deeper underlying philosophical issues. Methods are ultimately based on, and derive from, paradigms. Conversely, paradigms have implications for methods. This point became clear during methodological developments of the past 40–50 years. At this point, therefore, a brief sketch of some historical background on methods and paradigms in social research is appropriate.

Beginning in the 1960s, the traditional dominance of quantitative methods, as *the* way of doing empirical social science research, was challenged. This challenge accompanied a major growth of interest in using qualitative methods, and this in turn produced a split in the field, between quantitative and qualitative researchers. A prolonged quantitative–qualitative debate ensued, sometimes described as the 'paradigm wars'.

Much of that debate was characterized by either–or thinking. Some thought that only quantitative approaches should be used in research. Others were just as emphatic that only qualitative approaches are appropriate. More recently, however, there have been moves towards a detente, and an increased interest in the combination of the two approaches (Bryman, 1988, 1992; Hammersley, 1992; Tashakkori and Teddlie, 2010). This has led to mixed methods, a major growth area in more recent research methodology literature (Creswell and Plano Clark, 2007). These methodological changes have occurred across most areas of empirical social science research, though in some areas the changes have been more pronounced than in others.

The full story of these developments and debates is more complex than this. I have focused only on one main dimension of it, the quantitative–qualitative distinction, because these remain two of the central methodological approaches in social science research today. A major consequence of these developments is that qualitative research methods have moved much more into the mainstream of social science research, compared with their marginalized position of 40 or so years ago. And as noted, a further development has been the combination of the two approaches in what is now called 'mixed-method research'. As a result, the field of research methodology in social science is now bigger and more complex than it used to be.

Because of the connections between methods and paradigms, the history briefly outlined above also has a deeper level, a level that is not just about the quantitative–qualitative debate, or about research methods, but about paradigms themselves. On this deeper level, a major rethink began some time ago and is ongoing. It has brought a questioning of all aspects of research (its purposes, its place and role, its context, and conceptualizations of research itself) as well as the methods it uses. It has also brought the development of new perspectives, and of new approaches to data and to the analysis of data, within qualitative research especially. Prominent features of this rethink are the detailed critique of **positivism**, and the emergence and articulation of several different paradigms as alternatives to positivism. As a result, paradigm issues are in a state of change and development, and many matters are still contested.

It is the development of qualitative methods that has exposed the many different paradigm possibilities, and the situation has now become very complicated. Thus Denzin and Lincoln (2013 identify four main alternative inquiry paradigms underlying qualitative research (positivism, post-positivism, critical theory constructivism), but more detailed examples and classifications of paradigms are given by Guba and Lincoln (2013). Morse (2013) has this classification of paradigms with associated qualitative research strategies: philosophy–phenomenology; anthropology–ethnography; sociology–symbolic interactionism–**grounded theory**; semiotics–**ethnomethodology** and **discourse** analysis. Janesick (1994) has a more detailed list of paradigm-related qualitative research strategies, noting that it is not meant to include all possibilities: ethnography, life history, oral history, ethnomethodology, case study, **participant observation**, field research or field study, naturalistic study, phenomenological study, ecological descriptive study, descriptive study, symbolic interactionist study, microethnography, interpretive research, action research, narrative research, historiography and literary criticism. And examples of paradigms considered by writers in the philosophy of education are logical empiricism and post-empiricism, critical rationalism, critical theory, phenomenology, hermeneutics and systems theory.

This can be confusing and daunting territory for the beginning researcher, partly because of philosophy and partly because of terminology. Fortunately, in the light of these complications, some of the literature now seems to be converging and simplifying. In one version of this convergence and simplification, the main paradigm positions are positivism and interpretivism, in another they are positivism and constructivism. Thus, we have:

- positivism (associated mostly with quantitative methods), and
- either interpretivism or constructivism (associated with qualitative methods).

These associations – positivism with quantitative methods and interpretivism/constructivism with qualitative methods – are generally true, but they are not necessary associations. It is more accurate to say that positivism is likely to be associated with quantitative methods, and interpretivism and constructivism are likely to be associated with qualitative methods.

These terms are defined slightly differently by different writers, but their main nature-of-reality ideas are as follows:

- Positivism – the belief that objective accounts of the world can be given, and that the function of science is to develop descriptions and explanations in the form of universal laws; that is, to develop nomothetic knowledge.
- Interpretivism – the central reality in studying people and their behaviour concerns the meanings people bring to situations and behaviour, and which they use to make sense of their world (O'Donoghue, 2007); these meanings are essential to understanding behaviour.

- Constructivism – realities are local, specific and constructed; they are socially and experientially based, and depend on the individuals or groups holding them (Guba and Lincoln, 2013).

Question–method connections are an important aspect of the internal validity of any piece of research, and there needs to be compatibility and integrity in the way the research questions and research methods fit together in a study. This is shown in the top line in the diagram below. Paradigms expand that, because paradigms have implications both for the sorts of research questions asked and the methods used to answer them. This is shown in the bottom line in the diagram:

$$\text{questions} \longrightarrow \text{methods}$$

$$\text{paradigms} \longrightarrow \text{questions} \longrightarrow \text{methods}$$

What does all this methodological theory mean for planning and executing a piece of research? Broadly, there are two main ways planning a research project can proceed:

1. Paradigm-driven approach – one way is to begin with a paradigm, articulate it and develop research questions and methods from it.
2. Pragmatic approach – the other way is to begin with research questions that need answers and then choose methods for answering them.

In the pragmatic approach, the questions may come from any source – the literature, existing substantive theory, the media, personal experience, and so on. But very often, especially in professional fields such as education, management or nursing, they will come from practical and professional issues and problems associated with the workplace. The starting point here is not a paradigm. Instead, the starting point is a problem that needs solution or a question that needs answers; this is a pragmatic approach. To choose the pragmatic approach is to start by focusing on what we are trying to find out in research, and then to fit methods in with this.

This has sometimes been a contentious issue in higher-degree research programmes in social science areas. Some university departments have taken the view that paradigm issues are paramount, and insist that a piece of research should not be allowed to proceed until it has articulated its paradigm position. I believe this insistence is not well placed, because paradigm-driven research is not the only way to proceed, and because I see a big role for a more pragmatic, applied and professional approach to social science research. I have no objection to paradigm-driven research. My objection is only to the view that *all* research must be paradigm-driven. I take a similar view with respect to the philosophical issues involved in paradigm debates. I think we should be aware of the issues involved, and of the areas of debate. But we can proceed to do research, and to train researchers, mindful of those debates yet not engulfed by them, and without necessarily yet being able to see their resolution. In other words, we can acknowledge the connections of methods to these deeper issues, and discuss them from time to time as they arise, without making them the major focus of our research. This is to take the pragmatic approach noted, consistent with the view that not all questions for social research are driven by paradigm considerations, and that different sorts of questions require different methods for answering them.

5.3 METHODOLOGY VERSUS METHODS

These terms sometimes cause confusion, and are often used in different ways by differ-ent writers. To add to the confusion, they are sometimes used interchangeably, to mean the same thing. This section gives definitions of these terms, and clarifies the difference between them.

Methods are the specific techniques and tools used in research. Thus 'methods' is a narrow and specific term. A 'methods section' contains information at a very specific level.

Examples of different qualitative methods are comparative case study designs, in-depth interviewing, extreme case sampling, and **open, axial** and **selective coding**. Examples of different quantitative methods are Likert scaling in a survey questionnaire, different types of probability sampling such as random sampling, stratified random sampling or cluster sampling, **correlation** analysis and multiple **regression** analysis.

Methodology, on the other hand, is a broad term. On the most general level, methodol-ogy means the study of methods. The suffix '-ology' denotes a branch of knowledge, so methodology refers to the branch of knowledge concerned with methods. This includes the philosophical assumptions underlying different methods. Therefore, when applied to dissertation research, 'methodology' includes both the theoretical underpinnings and the overall framework and research strategy within which the different specific methods are to be used. Thus methodology is a much broader and more general term than meth-ods. It will normally include an identification and brief description of the paradigm informing the research.

Here is an example of summary description of methodology for a qualitative study:

> This qualitative study uses the interpretive paradigm – and symbolic interaction-ism in particular – to investigate teachers' perceptions of the value of real-world fieldwork in the teaching of secondary school geography. It will collect interview and documentary data from a deliberately chosen **sample** of teachers, and will use grounded theory methods of data analysis to analyse the data.[1]

---

[1]Reproduced by permission of Suzanne Johnson, Australian International School, Singapore.

By contrast, and in line with the methodological history outlined earlier in this chapter, quantitative research, being historically dominant, typically was not concerned with paradigm issues. Positivism was the implicit dominant paradigm, and for the most part, positivistic approaches to the research were taken for granted. Thus it would be unusual to see a description of the methodology for a quantitative study which began with the identification of positivism as the guiding paradigm. Despite this, it is true that positivism was – and is – the guiding paradigm behind most quantitative research, even if it is implicit.

I find a common problem is the use of the term 'methodology' when methods are being described. An indication of this is a section or chapter in a dissertation titled 'methodology', but with no mention in that section or chapter of paradigm issues, or of the theoretical underpinnings of the methods used. To me, this indicates a misunderstanding of the meaning of 'methodology'.

One implication of these definitions of methods and methodology flows from the distinction noted above between paradigm-driven research and pragmatic research. When paradigm-driven research is being proposed, it is both appropriate and necessary that the paradigm be identified, briefly described and then used to inform research questions and methods. On the other hand, when pragmatic research is being proposed, methodological issues of methodology – in the sense of paradigms – may not be relevant. Of course methods themselves still need to be identified and described, and it remains true that the methods proposed are ultimately based on assumptions and philosophical considerations, whether or not that is acknowledged and described.

5.4 SUBSTANTIVE THEORY

Section 5.2 used the term 'methodological theory' to refer to a particular paradigm or perspective which might inform a piece of research. This present section is about 'substantive theory' and the role it might play in the research. By substantive theory I mean a theory about a substantive issue or phenomenon, some examples of which are shown below. Usually, the function of such a theory is both to describe and to explain; an explanatory theory is one which not only describes but also explains the phenomenon of substantive interest. Thus theory, in this sense, is a set of propositions which together describe and explain the phenomenon being studied. These propositions are at a higher level of abstraction than the specific facts and empirical generalizations (the data) about the phenomenon. They explain the data by deduction, in the if–then sense.

Like methodological theory, the question about the role of substantive theory in a piece of research is sometimes considered more appropriate at the doctoral level than at the master's level. This seems to be because a common criterion among universities for the award of the doctorate centres on the 'substantial and original contribution to knowledge' the study makes, and the 'substantial' part of that criterion is often interpreted in terms of substantive theory.

Some examples of substantive theories from different areas of social science research are attribution theory, reinforcement theory, various learning theories and personal construct theory (from psychology); reference group theory and social stratification theory (from sociology); the theory of vocational personalities and career anchors (from occupational sociology); theories of children's moral development and of teacher career cycles (from education); and various leadership theories (from management and administration).

Thus, the general question at this point, for the research proposal, is 'What is the role of (substantive) theory in this study?' We can look at this question under two related questions:

- Does the description–explanation distinction apply in the proposed project?
- Does the distinction between theory verification and theory generation apply?

5.4.1 Description versus explanation

Does the description–explanation distinction apply in the proposed study? This is one of those issues which does not necessarily apply to all studies, but is nonetheless a useful question to consider when designing the proposal.

Research, whether quantitative or qualitative, can be descriptive, or explanatory, or both. A *descriptive study* sets out to collect, organize and summarize information about the matter being studied. To describe is to draw a picture of what happened, or of how things are proceeding, or of what a situation or person or event is (or was) like, or means, or of how things are related to each other. It is concerned with making complicated things understandable. In social science, it often involves summarizing specific factual information into empirical generalizations (if the research has a nomothetic or generalizing bias), or summarizing details of events, characteristics, cases or processes (if the research has an ideographic or particularizing bias).

An *explanatory study,* on the other hand, sets out to explain and account for the descriptive information. It too is concerned with making complicated things understandable, but on a different level. It aims to find the reasons for things, showing why and how they are what they are.

Description is a more restricted purpose than explanation. We can describe without explaining, but we cannot really explain without describing. Therefore explanation goes further than description; it is description plus something else. Broadly speaking, an explanatory study will be concerned with testing or verifying theory, or with generating theory, or with both of these.

One way to see the difference between description and explanation is to compare 'what' questions with 'why' or 'how' questions. A descriptive study asks, basically, 'What is the case or situation here?' An explanatory study asks, basically, 'Why is the situation here the way it is?' or 'How does (or did) this situation come about?' This description–explanation distinction applies to both quantitative and qualitative studies. For qualitative research, Maxwell (2012) has a third category of questions: interpretive questions. Thus descriptive questions ask 'what', explanatory question ask 'why', and interpretive questions ask about the meanings of things for the people involved.[2]

Both descriptive and explanatory studies have their place in research, and one is not necessarily better than the other. Rather, it is a question of assessing the particular research area or situation, and especially of assessing what stage the development of knowledge in that area has reached, and designing the emphasis of the study accordingly. Thus, for a relatively new research area (for example, how teachers use the internet in classrooms), it makes sense for research to have a descriptive emphasis. For a well-worked research area (for example, the relationship between social class and scholastic achievement), where considerable descriptive information already exists, it makes sense for research to have an explanatory emphasis.

In some quarters, however, the value of a purely descriptive study might be questioned. There may well be a view, especially at the doctoral level, that a study should try to do more than 'just describe'. There is a good reason for this: explanatory knowledge is more powerful than descriptive knowledge. When we know why (or how) something happens, we know more than just what happens, and we can use the explanation for prediction. But, as a counter to that, and in addition to the example of a new research area given above, a valuable step towards explanation can often be a careful and thorough description. A good first step in explaining why something happens is to describe exactly what happens. And careful descriptive work can be of great assistance in the development of more abstract concepts important in later theorizing. Also, some areas or styles of research have a different view on the merits of a descriptive study. An example is ethnography in anthropology (and in some applied social research areas), where 'full ethnographic description' may be the goal of the research. Another is Glaser's view of the Strauss and Corbin approach in grounded theory: that it is not true grounded theory, but rather 'full conceptual description' (see especially Glaser, 1992).

Explanation itself is a complex philosophical concept. The view of explanation I am using here emphasizes induction from specific facts or empirical generalizations to more general and abstract propositions. The empirical generalization is then a specific example of the more general proposition, which thereby 'explains' it. Another frequent and useful, but different, form of explanation is the 'missing links' form. Here, an event or empirical generalization is explained by showing the links which bring it about.

---

[2]More completely, Maxwell (2012) defines five categories of understanding in qualitative research: description, interpretation, theory (explanation), generalization and evaluation. The first three categories include most types of questions that qualitative researchers develop.

Thus the relationship between social class and scholastic achievement might be explained by using cultural capital (Bourdieu, 1973) as the link between them. Or the relationship between social class and self-esteem might be explained by using the parent–child relationship as the link between them (Rosenberg, 1968: 54–82).

To summarize, the questions for proposal development are:

- Is the proposed study descriptive, explanatory or both? In other words, does it aim to answer questions about 'what', or also about 'why' and 'how'?
- What is the logic behind the position taken, and how does that logic flow through the proposal?

5.4.2   Theory verification versus theory generation

This is another issue which may apply unevenly across different social science areas. It is linked to the previous section through the concepts of explanation and explanatory theory. Broadly speaking, the two main possible roles for substantive explanatory theory in a study are testing theory or generating theory. The first is usually called **theory verification**; the second is **theory generation**. This theory verification–generation distinction cuts across the quantitative–qualitative distinction. A theory verification study can be quantitative or qualitative or both; so can a theory generation study. Either can be appropriate, depending on the research area, topic or context. Neither is better than the other. At the same time, it is historically true that theory verification studies in social science research have more often been quantitative, and theory generation studies have more often been qualitative.

To repeat, I am using 'theory' here in the sense of substantive explanatory theory. In this sense, a theory is a set of statements which explains facts (observations, findings or empirical generalizations). It is at a more abstract level than the facts themselves. There is an if–then connection between the theory and the facts: if the theory is true, then the factual statements follow. These factual statements are hypotheses to be tested in a theory verification study.

A theory verification study aims to test a theory or, more accurately, to test propositions (that is, hypotheses – see Section 4.7.3) derived from the theory. This has been a very common model in social science areas which have traditionally emphasized quantitative research (such as psychology and some areas of management and education). Such a study starts with a theory, deduces hypotheses from it, and proceeds to test these hypotheses.

A theory generation study aims to generate or develop a theory to explain empirical phenomena or findings. Such a study typically starts with questions, moves to data and ends with a theory. This has been a common model in some qualitative research, especially where grounded theory is favoured (for example, nursing research).

This theory verification–generation distinction is really a matter of emphasis in a study. A theory verification study often ends up in theory modification or generation, especially if hypotheses are not confirmed. Similarly, a theory generation study will naturally use the processes of verification (and falsification) in constructing the theory. But, while the two may naturally get intertwined in doing the research, it is a good idea for a study to be clear at the proposal stage as to which of the two is its main focus and objective.

A theory verification study has hypotheses for testing. Hypotheses are specific predictions about what is expected to be found in the data, paralleling research questions, and they should follow from (and be explained by) the theory. As noted earlier (Section 4.7.3), I see little point in having hypotheses without also showing the theory from which they follow.

Therefore the questions at proposal development stage are:

- If the purpose is explanatory, does the study focus on theory verification or theory generation?
- What is the logic behind this position and how does that logic flow through the proposal?
- If theory verification is the focus, what are the hypotheses and what is the theory behind them?

5.5 THE LITERATURE

All social science research has a relevant literature, and no research takes place in a vacuum. The proposal writer therefore needs to:

- identify the literature that is relevant to the study and to be familiar with it;
- locate the present study in relation to the literature;
- determine how the literature will be handled in the proposal and, later, in the dissertation.

Each of these points is now discussed.

5.5.1 Relevant literature

What literature is relevant to this project? In dealing with this question, reference to your research area, topic statement and general research questions is obviously a very good starting point. Basing your reading around your general research questions provides a way of organizing literature; some literature is centrally relevant, some is generally relevant, and some is background literature. Rudestam and Newton (2014) have a Venn diagram using these ideas to guide the construction of a literature review. If you concentrate first on the research literature – mostly to be found in research journals, conference papers and proceedings, and dissertations – connections to the relevant theoretical, historical and contextual literature will normally build quickly. Access to major research library is therefore important, as is access to dissertation abstracts; as Burton and Steane (2004: 128) point out, others have gone before you. Articles in research journals usually include a brief literature review, and dissertations a more extensive one.

Some points to remember about identifying the relevant literature are:

- Different research areas and topics will have different quantities of relevant literature. In some areas the volume of literature will be vast, in others relatively small.
- More than one body of literature might be relevant, especially if your topic cuts across more than one substantive area.
- The levels-of-abstraction issue often arises. Be careful of saying there is no relevant literature for your topic. This statement may be true at a specific level, but not at a more abstract level. Realize that connections to relevant literature may require you to raise the level of abstraction of your topic. Two examples of this are given in Box 5.2.
- As well as traditional literature searching methods, the internet today is an indispensable resource for locating relevant literature.

BOX 5.1

Using the Literature: Levels of Abstraction

Raising the level of abstraction of a specific topic helps to show its connections with the literature. As an example, assume that the specific topic for the research is the educational performance of Aboriginal children in Narrogin, Western Australia. In all probability there is no literature or previous research on this specific topic. However, Aboriginal children are an indigenous ethnic minority group; Narrogin is a rural community. Now the search for relevant literature is broader: the educational performance of indigenous ethnic minority children in rural communities. Considerable research from different countries around the world is now relevant.

Bryant (2004: 65) expresses a similar idea in the following tip:

Realize that if you choose to study a tiny subset of a population in a very specific setting, this does not mean you should neglect the research about your topic that may have been carried out for other populations in other settings. For example, studying the leadership behaviours of Hispanic men in small non-profit organizations in a single county in a single state does not mean you do not need to inform your readers about leadership behaviours in non-profit organizations generally and of Hispanic men in general.

5.5.2 Relationship between study and literature

What is the relationship of the proposed study to its relevant literature? This includes such questions as: where does the proposed study fit in relation to its relevant literature? What is its connection to that literature? How will the proposed research move beyond previous work or beyond what we already know?

There are several possible answers to these questions. For example, this study may fill a gap in the literature; it may sit in line with the main trends in the literature, seeking to extend these trends; it may take a quite different direction from those in the literature; it may aim to confirm, challenge or disconfirm other findings, as in a replication study; it may test or extend a theory from the literature; or it may use a theoretical framework or model from the literature. There are other possibilities as well, so the general question to be dealt with in the proposal is: 'What contribution will this study make to the literature?'

5.5.3 Using the literature

How will the proposed study deal with the literature? In particular, how will the argument being developed in the proposal use the literature?

There are different ways a study may deal with its literature, and different expectations may apply for the use of the literature in the proposal. For example:

- The literature may be fully reviewed in advance of the research; the full literature review is part of the proposal and is included or attached (reviewing literature is discussed in the next section).
- The literature may be reviewed, but the review has not been completed at proposal submission time; in this case, part of the review, a sample of the review, or themes to be used in the review, may be included with the proposal.
- The literature will be reviewed, analysed and incorporated as the study progresses, and perhaps especially when the study's data are being analysed and its findings are being discussed. An example of this is a grounded theory study. When this approach to the literature is proposed, it is worth giving a clear statement of it and justification for it, if only because of expectations sometimes held that the literature will be reviewed ahead of the research.

As to how the proposal itself uses the literature, one view on this matter is provided by Locke et al. (2011), when they write that the proposal writer should place the research question(s) – or hypotheses – in the context of previous work in such a way as to explain and justify the decisions made for the proposed study, especially with respect to how and why the research question or hypothesis was formulated in the present form, and why the proposed research strategy was selected. They see no other role for the literature *in the research proposal*, and regard the heading 'review of the literature' as inappropriate in a proposal. Similar advice comes from Maxwell (2012). Clearly, this has the benefit of shortening the proposal. On the other hand, there are certainly situations where a literature review is expected or required in the proposal, and in such cases it usually precedes the research questions or hypotheses. Thus, the student needs to check departmental expectations on the question of literature review in the proposal. The following comments apply to those situations where reviewing literature is required as part of proposal development. They also apply, of course, to the literature review in the dissertation itself.

5.6 REVIEWING LITERATURE

A good literature review demonstrates your mastery of your dissertation topic, and is much more than a summary of the relevant literature. While summarizing the literature is important, your review should go beyond mere summarizing in two main respects. First, reviewing the literature requires the building of an argument. This, in turn, requires a synthesis of the literature, not merely a summary of it. Second, your review is expected to be critical, especially with respect to research literature. This means routinely examining and critiquing the methods used in reported research, with special reference to the generalizability or transferability of research findings (Bryant, 2004: 80). It also means taking an analytical approach in dealing with literature (Brink and Wood, 1994: 58), and critically reflecting on its organization, completeness, coherence and consistency.

Summarizing literature as you read is an important first step. Doing it systematically, with complete bibliographic details and organized filing, always pays later dividends, and it is wise to invest time early in your reading in developing an organized filing system. Once a sufficient overview of the relevant literature is achieved, summarizing needs to lead to the integration and synthesizing of literature. Burton and Steane (2004: 131) use the useful metaphor of tapestry to illustrate the idea of synthesizing literature, stressing the weaving together and integration of threads contained in previous writing on the topic. Synthesizing involves the convergence and divergence of findings, theories and implications, and Burton and Steane (2004: 131–2) further suggest the dialectical process of thesis–antithesis–synthesis as a framework for developing synthesis in a literature review.

Developing an organizing framework for dealing with the literature, as it is located and read, is part of reading critically and analytically, and the organizing framework you develop will often help with your own study's conceptual framework. It will also help to make your ultimate literature review both thematic (rather than merely a serialized or chronological summary of what others have done) and integrated with your study. Your study needs to be connected to its literature, so that there is some point to the literature review.

It is best to avoid unintegrated chronological summaries; a literature review is not the same as an annotated bibliography.

A complete literature review needs a structure; the alternative to a structured review is an amorphous mass of unstructured writing, which makes it difficult for the reader to navigate and comprehend. Integration and synthesis of the literature will normally suggest a structure for writing the review. Thus, sections and subsections within the review are useful, but should not be overdone. Also useful, and strongly recommended, is a short 'advance organizer' for the reader. Here the writer briefly describes the structure of the literature review to come, providing the reader with a 'road map' for navigating the material. Similarly important is how the literature review is finished off. Sound advice here is to lead back to the purpose and research questions of the study, showing at the same time how the present research relates to the literature just reviewed.

Good literature reviews are extremely valuable, tying a field together and showing the state of knowledge in an area, its trends and its gaps. They show 'where things are up to' in that area, what we already know and, just as important, what is contested and what we do not know. They are also difficult and time-consuming to do. Therefore, if you find a good literature review, my advice is to use it, of course with appropriate acknowledgements. In some research areas, the literature review will need to be selective. For some topics, the volume of related literature is so great that a dissertation literature review cannot be comprehensive, covering everything. In these cases, the researcher is forced to be selective. When that occurs, the writer should indicate the basis on which the selection is made, and why it is being done. This is where previous reviews of the literature, if available and relatively contemporary, can be extremely valuable. It is worth remembering that completed dissertations normally contain a literature review. Finding a recent dissertation on (or close to) your topic can save you a lot of time and work.

Finally, there are some pitfalls to avoid in compiling a literature review. Box 5.2 shows four common problems.

BOX 5.2

In Reviewing Literature, be Careful *not* to:

- *Quote in excess*. Judgement, experience and the reactions of supervisor(s) about the amount of quoting are useful, but too many direct quotes, or direct quotes that are too long, raise doubts about your mastery of the literature. Rudestam and Newton (2014: 59) have good advice. 'Restrict the use of quotations to those with particular impact or those that are stated in a unique way that is difficult to recapture.'
- *Rely too much on secondary sources*. At this level of work, you are expected, where possible, to study primary sources. Secondary sources are acceptable where the primary

source is not available or accessible, or where the secondary source adds significantly to the discussion. Again, however, over-reliance on secondary sources raises doubts about your mastery of the literature for your topic.

- *Neglect practitioner-oriented literature.* While the research literature on your topic is obviously important, there is often practitioner-oriented literature which is relevant and useful. This applies particularly to fields such as business and management research where trade journals are important.
- *Give in to the temptation to include and report everything you know or have read.* Your review needs to be selective, on an appropriate basis. As Rudestam and Newton (2014: 59) put it, 'build an argument, not a library'.

5.7 REVIEW CONCEPTS

Paradigm   A set of assumptions about the world, and about what constitutes proper techniques and topics for inquiring into that world.

Methodological theory   Theory about methods, and the philosophical assumptions which (necessarily) underlie any set of research methods.

Substantive theory   Content-based theory, which aims to develop a set of internally consistent propositions to describe and explain a substantive phenomenon of interest.

Positivism   The philosophical position that objective accounts of the world can be given, and that the function of science is to develop descriptions and explanations in the form of universal laws – that is, to develop nomothetic knowledge.

Interpretivism   The philosophical position that people bring meanings to situations, and use these meanings to make sense of their world and to organize their behaviour.

Constructivism   The philosophical position that realities are local, specific and constructed, and are socially and experientially based, depending on the people holding them.

Methodology   A broad term which includes both the theoretical underpinnings and the overall framework and research strategy within which the different specific methods are used.

Methods   A narrow term which means the specific tools and techniques used in a piece of research.

Description   Using data to draw a picture of a situation, event, person (people), or something similar; focuses on *what* is the case.

Explanation   Accounting for a description, showing why and how events or situations have come to be what they are; focuses on *why* (or *how*) something is the case.

Theory verification research   Research which sets out to test a theory, by testing hypotheses derived from the theory; begins with theory.

Theory generation research   Research which starts with research questions and data, and aims to build a theory to explain the data; finishes with theory.

──────── **EXERCISES AND STUDY QUESTIONS** ────────

1. What is a paradigm? What are the three main dimensions of paradigms?
2. How are paradigms and methods connected?
3. What is a paradigm-driven approach to research? What is a pragmatic approach to research? How do they differ?
4. Is the research you are planning paradigm-driven or pragmatic? How do you know – that is, how can you justify your answer?
5. What would a description of the climate of (say) a typical London winter's day look like? What would an explanation of that description look like? How are they different?
6. Is the research you are planning focusing on description, or explanation, or both? Why?
7. For what sorts of topics and research questions would prestructured research be appropriate?
8. For what sorts of topics and research questions would unfolding research be appropriate?
9. What are three purposes of a literature review in a dissertation? What is the role of a literature review in a proposal?
10. What does it mean to be critical in a literature review, and why is it important?
11. Find a literature review on a topic you are interested in in any recent review journal in your area of social science. Analyse the review, focusing on its structure, its level of critical assessment, its degree of analysis and synthesis, and its usefulness to researchers in the field.

6

PRESENTING
METHODS AND
METHODOLOGIES

6.1 INTRODUCTION

Let us assume at this point in the research planning process that we now have a stable set of specific research questions, connected with each other, integrated with general research questions and forming a coherent whole, and satisfying the empirical criterion. Let us assume also that the type of research, paradigm-driven or pragmatic, is also clear. The proposal can now deal with the methods for the research. In other words, since we now know what data will be needed, we can focus on how to get the data, and on what to do with the data once collected.

This chapter does not describe research methods in detail. Rather, I deal now in general terms with the four main methods issues any piece of research must deal with, once it has settled on its research questions: *strategy and design*; *sample and sampling*; *data collection*; and *data analysis*. The question throughout this chapter is: *what needs to be said about each of these four matters in the proposal?*

Before looking at these four issues in the light of this question, I look again at the overriding question of quantitative data, qualitative data or both.

6.2 QUALITATIVE, QUANTITATIVE OR MIXED METHODS?

Obviously, this is a fundamental issue of design and method, and a major organizing principle for the methods section of the proposal. Sometimes the logic of a study, including the way research questions (or hypotheses) are framed, is clearly qualitative or clearly quantitative, and that logic flows through naturally into the design, sampling, data collection and data analysis.

As a qualitative example, perhaps the research has been conceptualized as an ethnographic case study, focusing on interpretations, meanings and the cultural significance of some behaviour. Clearly, this involves qualitative data. As a quantitative example, perhaps the conceptualization of the problem and questions in the proposal is in terms of an experimental comparison, based on some intervention or treatment, with clear outcome variables in mind. This clearly involves quantitative methods and data. Or, as a mixed-method example, perhaps a quantitative survey is to be followed by qualitative interviewing.

Sometimes, however, the researcher can get to the point of having research questions, and of now having to confront methodological issues, without clear implications from what has gone before about whether the data should be qualitative or quantitative. In other words, the research could be done either way. Hence the question arises: qualitative data (and methods), quantitative data (and methods), or both? Here are six suggestions for dealing with this choice:

● Re-examine the research questions and the way they are phrased: what implications for data are there?

- Are we interested in making standardized comparisons, sketching contours and dimensions, quantifying relationships between variables and **accounting for variance**? These imply quantitative methods and data. Or are we more interested in studying a phenomenon or situation in detail, holistically and in context, focusing on interpretations and/or processes? These imply qualitative methods and data.
- What guidance do we find from the literature about this topic on this methodological question?
- What are the practical consequences of each alternative (including access to data and the need for resources)?
- Which way would we learn more?
- Which sort of research is more 'my style'?

Very often the question (qualitative or quantitative?) focuses entirely on the data themselves, in which case it really becomes: to measure or not to measure? This is because **measurement** is the process of turning data into numbers, and is therefore the operation which differentiates quantitative data from qualitative data.

Often, too, this matter is the subject of some misconceptions, where students feel they must (or must not) develop or use measuring instruments. I strongly prefer a common-sense answer to the question 'to measure or not to measure?' based on an understanding of what measurement is, and of how it can help us in answering research questions and in building knowledge. When looked at this way, I think there are many 'ambiguous'[1] empirical research situations where measurement helps.

Dealing with this commonly occurring and often perplexing question ('qualitative or quantitative data?' or 'to measure or not to measure?') is often made easier by remembering these four practical points:

- Get the research questions clear.
- As far as possible, let questions dictate the nature of the data.
- Measure if it is feasible and helpful to do so.[2]
- Use both types of data, if appropriate.

Thus any proposal needs to be very clear on the extent to which the research will:

- use qualitative methods and data;
- use quantitative methods and data;
- combine the two types of methods and data in a mixed-method study.

---

[1]'Ambiguous' in the sense that the research question(s) could be addressed using either quantitative or qualitative data.

[2]The distinction between the measurement of 'major' variables using established instruments, and measurement using researcher-constructed, ad hoc rating scales, is useful here (see Punch, 2011: 87–90).

If it combines the two approaches, it should be clear on which research questions involve qualitative methods and data, which involve quantitative methods and data, and which involve both. It should also be clear on the sort of combination that will be involved, given the various different models as to how mixed-method research can be done (Creswell and Plano Clark, 2007; Tashakkori and Teddlie, 2010). It is important that a mixed-method study has a clear logic underpinning the way the two types of data will be used.

On this question ('qualitative, quantitative or both?'), perhaps more than any other issue, the proposal should demonstrate internal validity. Here, this means that its methods should match its questions, and the argument and logic of the proposal should be clear and internally consistent. In line with the passing of the paradigm wars and of the associated quantitative–qualitative debate, there is an increasing tendency in a number of social science areas to combine the two approaches, bringing the two types of methods and data together.

6.3   A FOUR-PART FRAMEWORK FOR METHODS

The methods proposed can be developed and described using a four-part framework:

- strategy and design;
- sample and sampling;
- data collection;
- data analysis.

Design assembles the methods that will be used, showing how they are organized to answer the research questions, and strategy is the logic behind that. Sample deals with who or what will be studied. Data collection describes how the data will be collected. Data analysis describes how the data will be analysed.

Strategy and design

A research project must have a design, and the design should be based on a strategy. In developing a research proposal, and especially in clarifying and communicating the proposal, I think it is helpful to identify and describe the strategy. The description here is a short, logical, non-technical description of the steps to be followed in answering the research questions. Design – a technical term – then formalizes that strategy. At the centre of the design of a study is its internal logic or rationale – the reasoning, or the set of ideas and steps, by which the study intends to proceed in order to answer its research questions. This is the strategy. Here are strategy and design examples for a qualitative study, and quantitative study, and a mixed-method study.

Qualitative example

A comparative case study design will be used to study the implementation of policy change in schools. School A is generally considered to have been very successful in the implementation, whereas it is generally acknowledged that implementation in School B has been difficult and troublesome. Documentary data, informal observational data, and both **focus group** and in-depth interview data will be collected from key leaders in both schools, and from samples of classroom teachers. Data will be analysed using the Miles and Huberman approach, with a view to developing explanatory propositions to account for the different outcomes of the implementation.

Quantitative example

This experiment aims to compare direct instruction with cooperative learning in secondary school physics. Two comparison groups of approximately 30 students each will be set up by random allocation of Year 10 physics students. One group will receive eight weeks of direct instruction for ten topics from the Year 10 secondary school physics syllabus. The other group will study the same topics using cooperative learning in the classroom. After eight weeks, the two groups will be tested on their knowledge of these physics topics.[3]

Mixed-method example

This mixed-method sequential explanatory design (taken from Creswell and Plano Clark, 2007: 87) consists of two distinct phases: quantitative followed by qualitative. In this design, the researcher first collects and analyses quantitative data. The qualitative data are collected and analysed second in the sequence and help explain, or elaborate on, the quantitative results obtained in the first phase. The second qualitative phase builds on the first quantitative phase, and the two phases are connected in the intermediate stage of the study. The quantitative data provide a general understanding of the research problem. The qualitative data refine and explain those statistical results by exploring participants' views in more depth.

In this discussion, the term 'research design' needs to be general enough to accommodate qualitative, quantitative and mixed-method approaches. This general idea of design is one of situating the researcher in the empirical world. It means connecting the research questions to data. Design sits between the research questions and the data, showing how the research questions will be connected to the data, and what tools and procedures will be used in answering them. Therefore it needs to follow from the questions, and to fit in with the data.

---

[3]Used by permission of Kok Pin Chia, Hwa Chang Institution, Singapore

The design is the basic plan for the research, and, as indicated, includes the ideas of strategy, who or what will be studied, and the tools and procedures to be used both for collecting and for analysing empirical materials. Thus there are four main questions for research design:

- What strategy will be followed?
- From whom will the data be collected?
- How will the data be collected?
- How will the data be analysed?

Whatever the strategy and design, the researcher needs to describe them procedurally as well as generically. 'Generically' means identifying the design in general terms – for example, case study, ethnography, survey or **quasi-experiment**. That description is necessary, but only part of what is required. 'Procedurally' means saying how the researcher will execute the general strategy. To quote Dreher (1994: 289):

> In general, terms such as ethnography, participant observation, grounded theory, and fieldwork are not useful to a reviewer unless they are described procedurally, in relation to the specific proposal. For example, participant observation is perhaps the most pervasive technique used in ethnographic designs, yet we know that the investigator cannot participate and observe everywhere at the same time. Methodological choices must be made about where and when observations take place. Although some of these decisions necessarily are made in the actual process of the research, from the emerging data, the investigator should be able to provide reviewers with a general outline of observations that is consistent with the problem being researched.

The point made in this quote in a qualitative context applies just as well to quantitative and mixed-method research strategies and designs.

Sample and sampling

Who or what will be studied? This question concerns sampling for the research. In this form, the question is very general, covering both quantitative and qualitative approaches. A less general form of the question (more biased towards quantitative studies) is: *from whom will the data be collected?*

All empirical research involves sampling: in the words of Miles et al. (2014), 'you cannot study everyone everywhere doing everything'. The researcher thus needs to think through the sampling aspects of the study in preparing the proposal. It is best if the sampling plan is seen as part of the internal logic of the study, rather than as an afterthought to be considered when data collection is close. This means it needs to fit into the study's logic, to follow from it and to be consistent with it. This is an overriding general principle about sampling, whatever type of research is involved. For the proposal, therefore, the researcher needs to see sampling as part of the planning process for the research, to select among sampling possibilities in line with the logic of the study, and to indicate the sampling plan in the proposal.

Data collection

How will the data be collected? This question asks about the instruments (if any) and procedures to be used in data collection.

We get quantitative data from counting, scaling or both, and quantitative data collection instruments will normally be involved. Quantitative data collection instruments are questionnaires, standardized measuring instruments, ad hoc rating scales or observation schedules. Whichever of these is involved, this question often arises in planning research: will I use an existing measuring instrument, or will I develop instruments (in whole or in part) specifically for this study? Either choice, or some combination of the two, can be acceptable, depending on the particular study. Each alternative has implications for what is included in the proposal, as indicated in Section 6.5. As well as instruments, the actual data collection procedures also need to be described – the question here is 'how will the instrument(s) be administered?'

Qualitative data are most likely to be words, which we get by asking (interviewing), watching (observation) or reading (documents), or some combination of these three activities.[4] Again, the procedures by which data will be collected using these methods need to be described, as is dealt with in Section 6.4.

The question of instruments for qualitative data collection is both more contentious and more difficult to summarize. There is a range of possibilities here. At one end of the range, the idea of an 'instrument' to collect qualitative data, with its connotations of standardization and quantification, is quite inappropriate. Instead, in this sort of research, the researcher is seen as the primary instrument for data collection and analysis. Qualitative data are mediated through this human instrument, rather than through other instruments (Creswell, 2013).

At the other end of the range, qualitative data collection instruments may begin to resemble quantitative ones. Examples would be the questionnaire for a qualitative

---

[4]In either approach, the proposal for the research may be to work (in whole or in part) with data that already exist. This is known as **secondary analysis** – the term used for the reanalysis of previously collected and analysed data. In such a case, the proposal should discuss instruments, procedures and sample as appropriate, in describing how the initial data were collected.

survey, where open-ended questions are involved, or the schedule for qualitative interviews, where standardization across respondents is involved. Here, the same question arises as above, namely: do I use instruments already developed, or will I develop my own for this research? It is more likely that the qualitative researcher will develop instruments than use those developed by others. But either way, similar considerations apply to the proposal. If others' instruments are to be used, their background and previous use should be sketched. If instruments are to be developed for this study, it is appropriate to indicate the steps to be followed in developing them.

Data analysis

How will the data be analysed? After strategy/design, sampling and data collection, the other main methods question concerns what will be done with the data once they have been collected. What methods of analysis will be used? How will the data be analysed to answer the research questions?

Quantitative data analysis involves statistics, with well-established and well-documented techniques. While expert advice may be needed here, the proposal should indicate which statistical techniques will be used. Methods for the analysis of qualitative data have been a rapidly developing field in the past 40 or so years, and there are now many different data analysis varieties and possibilities for qualitative research. For the proposal, you should indicate, at least in general terms, what analytic techniques you propose to use in order to analyse the data you will collect. For both types of data, the proposal should also indicate what computer programs (if any) will be used in the analysis. In my experience, data analysis is an area where students will often need to seek expert advice, because of the issue of methodological expertise.

The question of methodological expertise

A recurrent question now arises, for both qualitative and quantitative approaches: how much *methodological expertise* should the student researcher be expected to show at the proposal stage? By 'methodological expertise', I mean expertise in the methods or techniques proposed. This question is probably most acute and most visible at the data analysis stage, but it can involve other areas as well (for example, sampling, measurement, interviewing skills). Here are two examples:

- A qualitative study is proposed, with the objective of generating a substantive theory of the phenomenon being studied. The researcher, quite appropriately, proposes to use grounded theory as the main data analysis approach and technique. To what extent should we expect the researcher to know the technical aspects of grounded theory analysis at the proposal stage?

- A quantitative survey is proposed, focusing on the relationships between different variables, as in a **correlational survey**. The researcher, again quite appropriately, proposes to use multiple regression analysis as the main data analysis approach and technique. To what extent should we expect that the researcher should know the technical aspects of multiple regression analysis at the proposal stage?

Here again, different universities and departments may have differing views on this matter. It is wise, therefore, to check relevant expectations with the department where you work. My view on this now is different from the view I held some 25 years ago. Today (in contrast to then), I would not require the candidate to demonstrate methodological mastery of a technique at the proposal stage. If it can be demonstrated, well and good, but I believe it is unrealistic today to require it. However, as a minimum, I think it is reasonable at the proposal stage to require the candidate to:

- have thought about what is required for the data analysis stage of the work;
- have developed – perhaps with expert assistance – at least a general idea of what technique(s) would be required and how they would be applied;
- be able to show how that fits in with the overall logic of the study.

In other words, I think it is sufficient for the candidate's knowledge to be at a logical rather than a technical level *at the proposal stage*. I think that translates into a statement such as 'I can see that I will need such-and-such a technique (for example, grounded theory analysis or multiple regression analysis) to analyse my data, because it will answer my research questions by enabling me to identify abstract grounded core concepts around which a theory can be built (grounded theory), or by showing how these independent variables relate to the dependent variables (regression analysis)'. Such a statement can be made by a student who has not yet developed technical mastery of the data analysis method, but has a logical understanding of how it operates and where it can be used. Developing this logical level of understanding is important, and a significant part of the learning which should occur through proposal preparation.

In short, I think it is acceptable today for the student not to have developed technical mastery at the proposal stage, ahead of the research. My reasoning is that the student will develop that mastery on the way through the research, and should be able to demonstrate it after completing the research. But having said that, it is surely all to the good, and to be encouraged, if the student can develop technical mastery ahead of the research.

The next three sections of this chapter give more detail about the methods section for qualitative, quantitative and mixed-methods research proposals respectively. The material is presented in checklist question form, and the questions and points shown need to be taken in conjunction with the general points already made in this chapter about strategy and design, sample and sampling, data collection and data analysis.

6.4 METHODS IN QUALITATIVE RESEARCH

Strategy and design

- What is the design of the study? (for example, qualitative survey, case study, ethnography, grounded theory)
- What is the strategy behind the design? Has it been described?

Sample and sampling

- How big will the proposed sample be, and why?
- What will be its composition, and why?
- How will the sample be selected – that is, what is the sampling strategy and how does the sampling strategy fit with the overall logic of the research?

Data collection

If data are to be collected by interview:

- What type of interview (structured/unstructured/semi-structured; standardized/unstandardized) will be used, and why?
- How will the interview schedule be developed and pretested?
- Where and when will interviews take place?
- How will interviews be recorded?

If data are to be collected by observation:

- What type of observation (structured/unstructured/semi-structured; standardized/unstandardized) will be used, and why?
- If a structured observation schedule is to be used, will it be an existing instrument, or will it be developed for this study?

If it is an existing instrument:

- How, where, when and by whom was it developed?
- How has it been used in previous research?
- What is known of its **psychometric characteristics**, especially its **reliability** and **validity**?

If an instrument is to be developed as part of the study:

- What steps will the development go through?
- How will the instrument be pretested?

- How will its psychometric characteristics be established, especially its reliability and validity?

Whether interviews or observation are involved:

- What data collection processes will be followed?
- What steps will be taken to maximize the quality of the data?

If documentary data is involved:

- Which documents will be used, and why?
- Is sampling among documents involved? If so, what is the sampling strategy?

Data analysis

- How will the data be analysed?
- What computer programs (if any) will be used?

6.5 METHODS IN QUANTITATIVE RESEARCH

Strategy and design

- What is the design of the study? (for example, experimental, quasi-experimental, correlational survey)
- What is the strategy behind the design? Has it been described?

Sample and sampling

- How big will the proposed sample be, and why?
- What will be its composition, and why?
- How will the sample be selected – that is, what is the sampling strategy (**representative**, **purposive**, or both) and how does the sampling strategy fit with the overall logic of the research?
- What claims will be made for the generalizability of the findings?

Data collection

Instruments

What data collection instruments will be used? (questionnaires, standardized measuring instruments, ad hoc rating scales, observation schedules)

- Where will they come from?
- If existing instruments are to be used:

  - How, where, when and by whom have they been developed?
  - How have they been used in previous research?
  - What is known of their psychometric characteristics, especially their reliability and validity?

- If instruments are to be developed as part of the study:

  - What steps will the development go through?
  - How will the instruments be pretested?
  - How will their psychometric characteristics be established, especially their reliability and validity?

Procedures

- How will the data collection instruments be administered? (face-to-face, online, mail, telephone)
- When and where will the instruments be administered?
- How long will the data collection process take?
- What steps will be taken to maximize the quality of the data, including maximizing response rates?

Data analysis

- How will the data be prepared for statistical analysis?
- What statistical techniques will be used to analyse the data?
- What computer programs will be used?

6.6   METHODS IN MIXED-METHOD RESEARCH

In writing the methods section of a mixed-method research proposal, much depends on which model of mixed-method research is proposed. In general, however, the check-list questions shown in this chapter for quantitative data can be used to describe the quantitative methods involved, and the questions shown for qualitative data can be used to describe the qualitative methods involved. A particular issue for mixed-method research is how the two types of data will be combined. Again, much depends on the particular model proposed. Different mixed-method models have different implica-tions for how the two types of data might be combined. An excellent reference dealing with this question, and categorising the different mixed-method models that can be used, is provided by Creswell and Plano Clark (2007).

6.7 REVIEW CONCEPTS

Quantitative data   Data in the form of numbers.

Qualitative data   Data not in the form of numbers.

Internal validity   In this context, the extent to which the different components of the research fit together; sometimes called internal consistency.

Design   Connects research questions to data; assembles the proposed methods and shows how they will be used to answer the research questions.

Strategy   The logic behind the design.

Sample   The people (usually) from whom data will be collected; most often, a smaller group drawn from some larger population.

Sampling strategy   The logic by which the sample will be selected.

—————— EXERCISES AND STUDY QUESTIONS ——————

1. Write a short one-paragraph description of your proposed research strategy. Keep it non-technical, so that it can be understood by people not working in your field (use some friends or family members to test this). Be guided by these questions:

    - If the study is quantitative, which quantitative strategy is proposed?
    - If qualitative, which qualitative strategy is proposed?
    - If there is a combination of quantitative and qualitative approaches, what is the proposed mixture of strategies?

2. Make sure that the section on sampling in your proposal can answer these questions:

    - Who or what will be studied?
    - From whom will data be collected? And, whether quantitative or qualitative:

        o What is the sample plan?
        o How big will the sample be (and why)?
        o How will sample units be selected?

If your study is mixed methods, make sure these questions are answered for both the qualitative and quantitative parts.

3. In the section on data collection, consider these questions:

- How will I collect the data?
- If existing instruments are to be used, what is known about them?
- If data collection instruments are to be developed, what steps will be followed?
- If qualitative fieldwork is involved, what is the data collection plan for that?
- What data collection procedures will be used?
- How will these procedures ensure that data of the best quality will be obtained?

4. If data collection by interview is proposed, consider these questions:

- What type of interview will be used, and why?
- How will the interview schedule be developed and pretested?
- Where and when will interviews take place?
- How will interviews be recorded?
- How will the data be analysed? What computer packages will be used?

7

WRITING THE
PROPOSAL

7.1 INTRODUCTION

What should the research proposal as a finished product look like? What content should it include? What structure and sections might it have? This chapter deals first with these questions, bringing together what has been said in previous chapters, especially Chapter 6. It then comments on qualitative proposals, and discusses academic writing.

The description of the research proposal given in this chapter aims to be general enough to suit different social science areas, and to cover quantitative, qualitative and mixed-method approaches to research. It is written primarily with the dissertation student in mind, but it has application also to the non-university context.

Before the proposal's sections and structure are discussed, it is worth noting again four points from previous chapters:

1. Keep the framework of three overarching questions discussed in Chapter 4 in mind, since this will be what your readers are expecting your proposal to deal with. These are:

    (a) What is this research trying to find out, what questions is it trying to answer?
    (b) How will the proposed research answer these questions?
    (c) Why is this research worth doing?

2. Review again the important issues raised in earlier chapters. As noted, they are not necessarily all applicable in any one project, but they are useful things to think about in planning the research and preparing the proposal. They are:

    (a) the role of theory, both methodological and substantive;
    (b) prestructured versus unfolding research;
    (c) the relevant literature;
    (d) whether the study is to be quantitative, qualitative or both.

When they do apply, how they are dealt with in the proposal is a matter of judgement for the writer – for example, whether, as points, they need a separate section, or are interwoven throughout other sections.

3. Remember that the form and structure of the proposal are tied to its purpose: 'to explain and justify your proposed study to an audience of nonexperts on your topic' (Maxwell, 2012).

4. The proposal itself needs to be presented as an argument. Seeing it as an argument means showing its line of reasoning, its internal consistency and the interrelatedness of its different parts. It means making sure that the different parts fit together, and showing how the research will be a piece of disciplined inquiry. As an argument, the proposal should show the logic behind the proposed study, rather than simply describing the study.

In so doing, it should answer the question why this approach and design, and these methods, have been chosen for this study.[1]

7.2   PROPOSAL HEADINGS

To make the proposal clear and easy for the reader to follow, it will need an organizing framework or structure. This section gives a suggested set of headings for writing and presenting the research proposal, shown in Table 7.1. As indicated there, a table of contents, following the title page, is important in showing the structure, and in helping readers navigate the proposal.

A problem in suggesting a general set of headings for proposals is the variation in headings, format and length of required documents across different areas of university research. There appear to be two extremes in university practice. Some universities (and some degrees) have institution-wide requirements, where the proposal covers the same headings in all disciplines. Other universities (and degrees) have department- or area-specific requirements and headings.

Institution-wide formats are usually, and necessarily, more general. For example, they often use the broad heading 'aims' (or 'objectives'), rather than the more specific 'research questions' focus emphasized here. Again, the broad heading 'research plan' might be used, rather than the more specific term 'research methods'. Where these broader terms are required, the headings shown here in Table 7.1 can easily be clustered accordingly.

The focus in this book on empirical research in social science means that a common set of proposal headings should be broadly useful across areas. At the same time, there needs to be room for variability in proposal format, to reflect the variability in research approaches, while accommodating the general expectations a reader will have when reading the proposal. These headings address those expectations, but it follows that they are not necessarily the only sections or headings, nor is their suggested order the only one that could be used. Therefore, this description is not meant to be prescriptive, and the researcher should feel at liberty to vary this material as appropriate. But that should be done against the background of readers' expectations (see Chapter 2), and any

---

[1]Maxwell (2012) has an excellent example showing the structure of a dissertation proposal, as an argument with its own logic. Locke et al. (2011) suggest three useful questions which address the logic of the proposed research, its topic and research question: What do we already know or do? (The purpose here, in one or two sentences, is to support the legitimacy and importance of the question.) How does this particular question relate to what we already know or do? (The purpose here is to explain and support the exact form of questions or hypotheses that serve as the focus for the study.) Why select this particular method of investigation? (The purpose here is to explain and support the selections made from among alternative methods of investigation.)

Table 7.1 Checklist of headings for research proposals

- Title and title page
- Table of contents
- Abstract
- Introduction – area, topic, problem, purpose
- Research questions

  - General
  - Specific

- Theory, hypotheses and conceptual framework (if appropriate)
- The literature
- Methods

  - Strategy and design
  - Sample and sampling
  - Data collection – instruments and procedures
  - Data analysis

- Significance
- Ethical issues
- References
- Appendices

Notes

- In some types of research, the research questions would come after the literature section
- In some situations, sections on costs (budget), risk management and timetable are required

guidelines from your department and/or university. Even if these particular headings are not used, the content they point to should be contained in the proposal, in some clear, easy-to-follow format.

Some of these sections apply to both quantitative and qualitative research, whereas some are more directly applicable to one approach than the other. The writer's judgement is needed to decide which sections are appropriate, in which order, and which might be omitted or combined. But the full list is useful to think about in proposal preparation, and it is also useful for developing full versions of the proposal – where shorter versions are required, a good strategy is to prepare the full version, then summarize it. Also, the full version of the proposal, outlined here, will be useful when it comes to writing the dissertation itself.

It is easier in many respects to suggest proposal guidelines for a quantitative study, since there is greater variety in qualitative studies, and many qualitative studies will be unfolding rather than prestructured. An unfolding study cannot be as specific in the proposal about its research questions, nor about details of the design. When this is the case, the point needs to be made in the proposal. Unfolding qualitative proposals are discussed again in Section 7.3.

Some proposals require the definition of terms. This occurs when terms are used which may not be understood by people outside the field of study, or when specialized technical terms are used, or when there is a need to define one or more terms clearly so that misunderstanding does not occur (Creswell, 2013). Quantitative research in particular has a clear tradition of defining its variables, first conceptually and then operationally. Whether or not a separate section is required for any definition of terms is again a matter of judgement – it can often easily be incorporated into other sections. But the conceptual and operational definition of variables in quantitative research is often best done in a separate section, perhaps under methods.

In what follows, I make some comments about abstracts and introductions. In the other main sections (research questions, theory and hypotheses, literature, methods), I bring together the points made in earlier chapters.

7.2.1 Abstract and title

An abstract is a brief summary, whether of a proposal or a finished study. It is *not* the introduction to a proposal or study, but rather a summary of it. It functions like the executive summary in the business context, giving readers a brief overview of all essential elements of the proposal.

Abstracts play an important role in the research literature, and they are required in proposals (usually), in dissertations and in research articles in most refereed journals. Abstract writing is the skill of saying as much as possible in as few words as possible. For a proposal, the abstract needs to deal with two main issues: what the study is about and aims to achieve (usually stated in terms of its research questions), and how it intends to do that.[2] The abstract should give an overview, not just of the study itself, but also of the argument behind the study.

For most of us, abstract writing is a skill which needs to be developed, since we typically use many superfluous words when we speak and write. Together with the title, the abstract is written last, since it is difficult to summarize what has not yet been written.

Examples of abstracts of proposals are difficult to find, since they are not collected and published. On the other hand, examples of abstracts of completed studies can be found in several places – completed dissertations, at the start of articles in most peer-reviewed research journals, and in compilations of research such as *Dissertation Abstracts International*, and the various collections of abstracts in different social science areas.

---

[2]For a finished report (or dissertation), the abstract would need to deal with three issues – these two, and a third which summarizes what was found.

Titles are also important in the research literature indexing process. Therefore a title should not just be an afterthought, nor should it use words or phrases which obscure rather than reveal meaning. Extending the point about abstract writing, the title should convey as much information as possible in as few words as possible.

As noted, it is a good idea, immediately after the title page, to include a table of contents. Readers will need to 'navigate' their way through the proposal, and a table of contents provides the 'road map' to do so.

7.2.2   Introduction: area, topic, problem and statement of purpose

There are many ways a topic can be introduced, and all topics have a background and a context. These should be noted in the introduction, which sets the stage for the research. A strong introduction is important to a convincing proposal. It is the lead-in, to help the reader follow the logic of the proposal. Its purpose is not to review the literature, but rather to identify the area, topic and direction of the research, to show generally how the proposed study fits into what is already known, and to locate it in relation to present knowledge and practice. Creswell (2013) suggests four key components for introductions: establishing the problem leading to the study; casting the problem within the larger scholarly literature; discussing deficiencies in the literature about the problem; and targeting an audience and noting the significance of this problem for the audience.

The introduction should contain a clear identification of the research area and topic, and a general statement of the purpose of the research.[3] As noted earlier, showing how the problem behind the research leads logically to the purpose of the research gives the proposal internal validity, and becomes the basis of the proposal-as-argument. The general statement of purpose can then lead to research questions (general and specific). Particular features of the proposed study, and important aspects of its context, can also be identified here, as appropriate – for example, if personal knowledge or experience form an important part of the context, or if preliminary or pilot studies have been done, or if the study will involve secondary analysis of existing data (Maxwell, 2012).

Especially for qualitative proposals, two other points might apply here. One is the methodological theory issue raised in Chapter 5: is there a particular paradigm behind this research? If so, this can be noted here, to inform the reader early in the proposal. The other is the third issue raised in Chapter 2: where on the structure continuum is the proposed study? This strongly influences later sections of the proposal. If a prestructured

---

[3]Creswell (2013) gives examples of purpose statements for five different types of studies: a phenomenological study, a case study, an ethnographic study, a grounded theory study and a quantitative survey.

qualitative study is planned, the proposal can proceed along similar lines to a quantitative proposal. If an unfolding study is planned, where focus and structure will develop as the study proceeds, this point should be made clearly, again to inform the reader. In the former case, there will be general and specific research questions. In the latter case, there will be more general orienting research questions.

The introduction should be strong and engaging. Various logical structures are possible, but a progression from more general to more specific issues, culminating in stating the topic, problem, purpose and research questions for this study, often works well. Whatever structure you choose, make sure your introduction actually does introduce your topic, and sets the stage for what follows. In my experience, it is a mistake for the introduction to go on too long, especially about the background to the research, and it is a good idea to get to the point of your research, stated as problem and purpose in the introduction and leading on to research questions, as soon as possible.

An excellent illustration of an introduction, with edited comments, is given by Creswell (2013). Four others, also edited, are given in Locke et al. (2011), and others in Gilpatrick (1989: 57–60).

7.2.3   Research questions: general and specific

The nature and central role of research questions were discussed in Chapter 4. In the proposal outline suggested here, they can follow from the statement of purpose given in the introduction. If your research questions fit into the general-to-specific framework described in Chapter 4, presenting them in the proposal in this section should be quite straightforward. Remembering the empirical criterion for research questions in Section 4.6, it should be clear what data are required to answer each specific research question.

The point about this section is to tell the reader what questions the research is trying to answer, or what questions will initiate the inquiry in an unfolding study. This section is often what proposal readers turn to and concentrate on first, in order to get as clear a picture as possible of the purpose of the research. This reinforces the comments in Chapter 4 about the central role of research questions. It also implies that an emerging-unfolding type of study needs to indicate here what general questions will initiate the research, and how they might be refocused and refined as the study progresses.

7.2.4   Theory, hypotheses and conceptual framework

There is wide variation in the applicability of this section, given the range of studies possible across the qualitative, quantitative and mixed-method approaches. If a conceptual framework is involved, it is a matter of judgement whether it goes here, or in the methods section later in the proposal. Theory and hypotheses are included if appropriate, as explained in Chapter 4. If substantive theory is involved, it may be included in the literature review section, rather than here. Wherever it is placed, it should be made clear whether theory generation or verification is involved. If a theory verification study is proposed, hypotheses, and the theory behind them, should be shown.

7.2.5 The literature

The proposal needs to identify the body of literature which is relevant to the research, to indicate the relationship of the proposed study to the relevant literature, and to indicate how the literature will be dealt with in the proposed study. These three possibilities were noted in Chapter 5:

- The literature is reviewed comprehensively in advance of the study, and that review is included as part of the proposal, or is attached.
- The literature will be reviewed comprehensively ahead of the empirical stage of the research, but that review will not be done until the proposal is approved. In this case, the nature and scope of the literature to be reviewed should be indicated.
- The literature will deliberately not be reviewed prior to the empirical work, but will be integrated into the research during the study, as in a grounded theory study. In this case too, the nature and scope of the literature should be indicated.

For some proposals, the literature may be used in sharpening the focus of the study, and to give structure to its questions and design. If so, this should be indicated, along with how it is to be done. In all cases, the researcher needs to identify the relevant literature, and to connect the proposed study to the literature. In general, I agree with the advice of Locke et al. (2011) and Maxwell (2012) – that the function of the literature *in the proposal* is to locate the present study, and to explain and justify the directions it proposes to take.

7.2.6 Methods

Strategy and design

As indicated earlier, strategy here means the internal logic by which the study will proceed in order to answer its research questions. Design then formalizes that strategy, in more technical terms. Therefore a good way to start this section is with a short, non-technical summary of the study's strategy:

- If the study is quantitative, what strategy is proposed?
- If qualitative, what strategy is proposed?
- If there is a combination of quantitative and qualitative approaches in mixed-method research, what is the proposed mixture of strategies?

A clear statement of the strategy helps to orient the reader, shows the logic of the research and leads naturally to a description of the design.

The design sits between the research questions and the data, and can now detail the implementation of the strategy. For example, if an experiment is planned, this section gives details of the proposed experimental design (for example, one factor or two factors, single or repeated measures, formation of comparison groups, the nature of any intervention ... and so on). If a case study is planned, this section gives details of the case study design (for example, single or multiple, cross-sectional or longitudinal ... and so on).

For conventional quantitative designs, the conceptual framework may be shown here, instead of earlier. In qualitative studies, the location of the study along the structure continuum is particularly important for its design. Qualitative strategies such as case studies, ethnography and grounded theory may overlap, or elements of these may be used separately or together. This means it will be difficult to compartmentalize such a study neatly. That is not a problem, but it should be made clear that the proposed study uses elements of different strategies. Qualitative studies vary greatly on the issue of pre-developed conceptual frameworks, and the position of the study on this matter should be indicated. A fully or partly predeveloped framework should be shown. Where one will be developed, it needs to be indicated how that will be done. This will interact with data collection and analysis, and may be better dealt with there.

Sample and sampling

Chapter 6 stressed the need to think about sampling in the study as part of the planning process for the research, to select among sampling possibilities in line with the logic of the study, and to indicate the sampling plan in the proposal. The rationale behind the sampling plan needs to fit in with the logic of the study, and to be briefly described. Whatever the approach, the basic idea in this section is to indicate who or what will be studied, and why.

If the study is quantitative, the proposal should indicate:

- the sampling strategy, especially whether it is purposive, representative or both, and what claims will be made for the generalizability of findings;
- how big the sample will be, and why;
- how it will be selected.

If the study is qualitative, the proposal should similarly indicate:

- the sampling strategy, including what intention (if any) there is for the generalizabilty of findings;
- the extent of the proposed sample;
- how sample units will be chosen.

If a case study is involved, the basis of case selection should be made clear, as should the basis of within-case sampling. If sampling of documentary or other qualitative material is proposed, the strategy for this needs to be shown.

Data collection

As indicated in Chapter 6, the two matters here are the instruments (if any) which will be used for data collection, and the procedures for administering the instruments or, more generally, for collecting the data.

Instruments

For quantitative data collection:

- If the decision is to use already existing data collection instruments, a brief description of their history, their use in research and their basic psychometric characteristics (especially reliability and validity information, if available) should be included.
- If the decision is to construct one or more instruments specifically for this study, an outline of the steps involved in doing that should be given, showing the pretesting and psychometric investigation involved.

For qualitative data collection:

- A general plan for any qualitative fieldwork should be shown. If the researcher is the 'instrument' for data collection, the proposal should indicate this.
- If interviews are involved, the type of interviews, and especially the degree of structure and standardization proposed, should be specified. If standardized interview schedules are to be used, how will they be developed and pretested?
- If qualitative questionnaires are proposed, what degree of structure and standardization is involved? How would they be developed and (if appropriate) pretested?
- Similar considerations apply for observational data – what degree of structure and standardization is proposed, and how would proposed schedules be developed and pretested?
- If documents are to be used, which ones and why? Are there sampling or access considerations?
- If diaries, journals, critical incident reports or other qualitative materials are involved, how would the collection of these, including any sampling aspects, be organized?

Procedures

For both quantitative and qualitative approaches, the proposal needs to indicate:

- how the data will be collected;
- how the proposed procedures are arranged to maximize the quality of the data.

Issues of access and ethics may be dealt with here, if they apply especially to data collection procedures, or in the section on ethical issues, if they apply more generally.

Data analysis

The objective in this section is to indicate how the data will be analysed. Quantitative proposals should indicate the statistical procedures proposed. Similarly, the qualitative proposal needs to show how its data will be analysed, and how the proposed analysis fits with the other components of the study. If applicable, both types of proposal should indicate what computer use is planned in the analysis of the data. As noted in Chapter 6, this is an area where you may well need the help of an expert.

7.2.7 Significance

Here, the proposal should indicate the significance of the proposed study. Synonyms for 'significance' here might be justification, importance, contribution or intended outcomes of the study. They all address the third general question of Chapter 4: why is this study worth doing? While the particular topic and its context will determine a study's significance, there are three general areas for the significance and contribution of a study: to knowledge in the area, to policy considerations and to practitioners (Marshall and Rossman, 2015). The first of these, contribution to knowledge, is closely tied to the literature in the area, and is often interpreted as theoretical contribution. If the study has the clear objective of theory generation or verification, indicating this contribution is straightforward.

7.2.8 Ethical issues

All social research involves consent, access and associated ethical issues, since it is based on data from people and about people. Some ethical issues are present in almost all projects (for example, anonymity and confidentiality of data, the use of results), while others are much more project-specific (for example, intervention and advocacy). The researcher needs to anticipate the particular ethical issues involved in the proposed project, and to indicate in the proposal how they will be dealt with. In addition, proposals need to comply with the ethics requirements of departments and universities where the research is being done, and there are ethics approval forms to be completed as part of this compliance. It is wise to study these forms, and the associated institutional requirements and processes, before finalizing the proposal. In addition, Chapter 3 lists and discusses important ethical issues which can arise in social research.

7.2.9 References

This is a list of the references cited in the proposal.

7.2.10 Appendices

These may include any of the following: letters of introduction or permission, consent forms, measuring instruments, questionnaires, interview guides, observation schedules, and examples of pilot study or other relevant work already completed (Maxwell, 2012).

7.3 QUALITATIVE PROPOSALS

Qualitative studies vary greatly, and in many the design and procedures will evolve. This obviously means that the proposal writer cannot specify exactly what will be done, in contrast to many quantitative proposals. When this is the case, the proposal can explain the flexibility the study requires, and show how decisions will be made as the study unfolds. Together with this, as much detail as possible should be provided. Review committees have to judge both the quality, feasibility and viability of the proposed project, and the ability of the researcher to carry it out. The proposal itself, through its organization, coherence and integration, attention to detail and conceptual clarity, can inspire confidence in the researcher's ability to execute the research.

On the one hand, then, for some types of qualitative research especially, we do not want to constrain too much the structure of the proposal, and we need to preserve flexibility. On the other hand, this does not mean that 'anything goes'. Eisner (1991: 241–2) writes as follows about qualitative research in education:

> Qualitative research proposals should have a full description of the topic to be investigated, a presentation and analysis of the research relevant to that topic, and a discussion of the issues within the topic or the shortfalls within the research literature that make the researcher's topic a significant one. They should describe the kinds of information that are able to be secured and the variety of methods or techniques that will be employed to secure such information. The proposals should identify the kinds of theoretical or explanatory resources that might be used in interpreting what has been described, and describe the kind of places, people, and materials that are likely to be addressed.

> The function of proposals is not to provide a watertight blueprint or formula the researcher is to follow, but to develop a cogent case that makes it plain to a knowledgeable reader that the writer has the necessary background to do the study and

has thought clearly about the resources that are likely to be used in doing the study, and that the topic, problem, or issue being addressed is educationally significant.

This elaborates Eisner's earlier comments that 'evidence matters' and 'planning is necessary'. I want now to develop these points further, focusing both on proposals for qualitative research in general, and on those with unfolding rather than prestructured elements in particular. This sort of proposal is probably the most difficult to write, but the following points can guide the writing. They fit in with the headings shown in Table 7.1, though some modifications are required.

First, there should still be an identification of the research area and topic, and an introduction to those which places them in context and describes any necessary aspects of the background to the study. Second, there still needs to be an identification of the relevant literature, a connection of the proposed study to that literature, and an indication of how the research itself will deal with the literature. Third, there needs to be a statement of the proposed study's significance and contribution, including its contribution in relation to the literature.

Fourth, when it comes to research questions, it is likely that only general guiding and starting research questions will be identified in such a proposal, supported by statements as to why this is appropriate and as to how more specific questions to direct the investigation will be identified as the research proceeds. As a matter of proposal presentation strategy, it is a good idea to indicate possible (or likely) research questions as the study unfolds, while pointing out that they are first approximations, to be revised and changed as the study proceeds. It is usually not difficult to make an intelligent first approximation to the sorts of research questions that might arise, through anticipating and trying to imagine or simulate the research situation. For some research also, small-scale empirical exploration (or pilot study) may be possible in developing the proposal. Where possible, this is very helpful in keeping things grounded.

Fifth, when it comes to methods, there should be clear statements in the proposal about the general research strategy envisaged, about the sorts of empirical materials to be targeted (at least initially), and about the general plan for collecting and analysing them. As before, the description of methods should not stop at a general identification of the research strategy. The proposal needs also to indicate awareness of the procedural and methodological choices ahead of the researcher in implementing the general strategy, and the basis on which those choices will be made. This was the distinction made in Section 6.3.1 between general and procedural descriptions of methods. Terms describing qualitative research strategies such as the case study, or participant observation, or grounded theory, or an interview-based study are necessary, but they are generic descriptions, identifying an approach and a strategy in general terms. The execution of any of these in research involves numerous procedural and methodological choices.

Thus the 'interview-based study', for example, involves choices about such matters as the selection of interview respondents, approaches to them, the establishment of trust and rapport, physical arrangements for the interview (time, place, etc.), recording procedures, the type of interview, the nature of the questions and the role (if any) of an interview schedule and pretesting. The qualitative proposal does not need to be able to answer all such questions. Indeed, many of them may well be unanswerable at the proposal stage. But the proposal should indicate awareness of such upcoming methodological choices, and the basis on which they will be made.

Sixth, the other proposal headings listed (abstract and title, ethical issues, references and appendices) apply, as appropriate, as before.

Writing the proposal for a qualitative study can be more complicated, given the less prestructured nature of most such research. The writer should indicate early in the document the unfolding nature of the proposed research and why such an approach is appropriate for this study on this topic in this context at this time. The need to preserve flexibility, the unfolding nature of the study, and the ways in which this research will follow a path of discovery can be strongly stated. Against that background, it is good advice to develop likely research questions and issues of design and methods as far as possible in the proposal, indicating what methodological choices will be involved and the basis on which they will be made.

7.4 ACADEMIC WRITING

Academic writing is required in proposals and dissertations for higher degrees in universities. Despite some discipline-specific conventions and preferences, there are widely held expectations for the general characteristics of academic writing, which are now briefly described.

Academic writing relies on logical argument, on the development and interconnection of ideas, and on internal consistency and coherence. For this reason, it depends heavily on well-organized paragraphs with topic sentences, which are appropriately interconnected with each other. Two things which stand out very clearly to the experienced reader of academic writing (especially of proposals and dissertations) are the lack of connection between different points and, even worse, the inconsistency between different points. Among other things, the need for the logical development and interconnection of ideas requires us to be careful about the overuse of dot or bullet points. Occasionally they are fine, for clarity and emphasis. But their overuse is a mistake – interconnected argument cannot be built using only separate points.

The language of academic writing for research purposes should be *dispassionate, precise* and *consistent*. 'Dispassionate' means that the purpose of academic writing in proposals and dissertations is to inform, not persuade. Thus your proposal is not the place to 'grind your axe', or to pursue your favourite hobby horse, or to persuade others about a conclusion you have already reached. For this reason, dispassionate and unemotional language is expected. 'Precise' means that accurate and unambiguous language is part of the careful approach which scholarship requires, with thorough attention to detail. In the same vein, conclusions should be based on evidence, and in line with academic honesty, the writer should clearly identify when speculation goes beyond evidence. 'Consistent' means that terms should be used in the same manner (as well as precisely). Avoid the substitution of one term for another when the same thing is meant by both terms. This can create confusion for the reader.

Similarly, academic writing in a scholarly context needs to be appropriately formal. This means avoiding slang, jargon and colloquialisms. It also means taking special care with – and not overdoing – the use of abbreviations and acronyms. Students often have a problem here. If the everyday discourse in the environment where they are working or studying makes heavy use of abbreviations and acronyms, there is the understandable temptation to write this way in the proposal. This, however, makes it difficult for the reader unfamiliar with that environment. A good rule is to write for the unfamiliar reader. Then acronyms and abbreviations can be used in full the first time they occur, with short forms thereafter. But even when that is done, an equally good rule is not to overdo the use of acronyms and abbreviations.

7.4.1   Strategies to help with academic writing

It is understandable that the beginning research student may see the prospect of writing a proposal – and later a dissertation – as formidable and daunting. The following four well-known strategies can help reduce the writing task from formidable to manageable:

1. Develop a structure for the document that has to be written. The structure will have sections and subsections, and, up to a point, the more detailed the structure the better. One way to do this is to plan a table of contents for your document early in the process of writing – it may need several versions, and can be revised as you proceed. Once you have sections and subsections, you have modularized your writing task. Instead of one formidable task (writing the proposal, or the dissertation), you now have a series of manageable ones (writing the introduction, or the literature review, or the data collection subsection of the methods section). This chapter has described a structure for writing the research proposal.
2. Set deadlines, both for the whole document, and for different main sections. Using the due date for submission of proposal or dissertation, first schedule time for revisions (see below). This gives you the date by which you need to have completed a first draft.

Then work backwards from that date to develop self-imposed deadlines for completing the draft of each main section.

3. If possible, write every day, preferably at the same time each day, for (roughly) the same length of time each day, and in the same place. This builds important conditioned associations between writing, and place and time of day. It also helps overcome the common problems of inertia, procrastination and writer's block.

4. When each daily writing session ends, make yourself a note about what to do next. This helps to deal with the problem of discontinuity – sitting down to write the next day, and spending the first period, usually in frustration, trying to pick up the threads from the previous session.

Together, these strategies can help you build writing momentum, which is necessary to get significant documents written. They also, by modularizing, make the task manageable. They should take you to a position of having a complete draft of your proposal with time for the necessary revisions.

It is important now to stress that academic writing requires revision. Every successful academic writer understands the importance of revising what is written. Put bluntly, when it comes to academic writing, nobody gets it right the first time. When you read good academic writing, you can be sure that it has gone through the revision process, and usually more than once.

The main tasks in the revision process will typically focus on tidying up the use of language (often shortening by removing unnecessary verbiage), attending to details of grammar, punctuation, format and presentation, ensuring internal consistency and building connections between the different parts. Once again, it is good to have a deadline for revisions. Sometimes, students without deadlines get trapped in endless cycles of revisions, in a fruitless quest for perfection.

Two other strategies can help, if circumstances permit. The first is the 'drawer treatment' (Cryer, 2006). This means putting a completed draft aside (in a drawer – or computer) for at least a few days, with the idea of returning to it refreshed and with a clearer view as final revisions are done. The second is to read your work aloud (Ward, 2002: 102). This helps you identify and correct sentences which are too long and complex, and other awkward structures. It also helps you to achieve writing which flows, and is therefore easier to read.

7.5   REVIEW CONCEPTS

Title   In as few words as possible, a brief description of the topic of the proposed research.

Abstract   Again, in as few words as possible, a brief description of the topic, purpose and research questions, and a brief overview of proposed methods.

Introduction   The first section of a proposal which informs the reader about the area, topic, problem and purpose behind the research, and puts these things into a background and context.

Theory (substantive)   In a proposal for hypothesis-testing research, the explanation behind the hypothesis or hypotheses.

Hypothesis   A predicted answer to a research question, and a proposition for empirical testing which follows from the theory.

Conceptual framework   A framework showing the central concepts of a piece of research, and their conceptual status with respect to each other.

Literature   In this context, previous work which is relevant to the proposed research; some literature will be centrally relevant, while some will be only marginally relevant.

Methods   A description of the specific methods to be used in the proposed research. Can be done using the four-part framework of strategy and design, sampling, data collection, data analysis.

Significance   A short section in a proposal which addresses the question why the research is worth doing (also called 'Justification', 'Importance' or 'Contribution').

Ethical issues   In this context, the issues, such as integrity, honesty, and respect, which will arise in the proposed research, and how they will be dealt with.

—————— EXERCISES AND STUDY QUESTIONS ——————

1. Write down your research questions (as best you see them at the moment). Try to restrict yourself to three or four general questions, each of which can have specific questions (see the general–specific research question distinction described in Chapter 4).
2. Write a description of the strategy you propose to use to answer your research questions. At this stage, avoid technical language – use everyday language to describe the set of steps by which you will answer the research questions. This description should be quite short – not more than one paragraph.
3. Try writing an introduction (2–3 pages) to your proposal. Keeping your research questions in mind, identify the area, topic, problem and purpose of your research. Put all of this in context, so that a reader can understand. (A useful hint for context is to work from general to specific.) See if you can finish your introduction by constructing a logical argument, leading to 'therefore the purpose of this research is to . . .'.
4. Use bullet points to indicate the specific methods you will use in the research. Under the four methods headings of strategy/design, sample, data collection and data analysis, list the methods you will use.
5. Again in bullet-point form, indicate the significance this research will have. Aim for statements such as: 'This research will be significant in (or will make a contribution in) X ways'.

6. Write a draft abstract summarizing the purpose, research questions and methods of your proposed research. Limit it to 200 words. When you have done that, reduce it to 100 words. (*Hint*: several drafts will be required here – nobody gets abstracts right the first time!)
7. Now write a title, telling the reader as much as possible in as few words as possible. Limit it to not more than 12 words. (Avoid unnecessary phrases such as 'A study of' or 'An investigation into'.)

8

GETTING TACTICS
RIGHT

8.1 INTRODUCTION

I believe there is no one way to develop a research proposal, and I have seen how much difference there is between the way different researchers proceed. But I have also found that some strategies and tactics are consistently useful, especially for student researchers coming to proposal development for the first time. This chapter presents these.

8.2 GENERAL TACTICAL ISSUES

Before discussing useful strategies and tactics, however, I restate five general tactical considerations which should stay in the proposal writer's mind throughout the process of proposal development. They follow on from what has been said in previous chapters.

1. Keep an overall focus on the three most general questions:

    (a) *What* am I trying to find out?
    (b) *How* am I going to do it?
    (c) *Why* is this worth doing?

2. Put the 'what' question before the 'how' question. As far as possible, make research methods dependent on research questions, rather than questions dependent on methods. Remember that how you ask questions has implications for the methods to use in finding answers to them.

3. Realize that you will almost certainly have to revisit both the 'what' and the 'how' questions several times before you get the proposal right. The process is an iterative one, whether the proposal is quantitative, qualitative or mixed-method. Whereas the research proposal, as a product, is expected to be neat, tidy, well structured and interconnected, showing clarity and internal consistency, the process is usually messy, iterative, stop–start, and often punctuated with tensions, hesitations and contradictions. The same is true of much of research itself.

4. The importance of feedback: throughout the process of putting your proposal together, you will need reactions and feedback from various quarters – friends, fellow students, and especially supervisors (see Section 8.4.2). Make it easy for them to give you feedback which helps. Two ways you can do that are to provide them with draft documents which are easily understood, and to raise directly with them – preferably attached to your drafts – questions and matters to which you would like their reaction.

5. Modularizing: student researchers are often daunted by the task of producing a finished research proposal. It can seem formidable. But, like other formidable tasks, it loses much of its sting when broken down into smaller, specific, component tasks. To do that requires an outline, and Chapter 7 suggests sections for that outline. Once the outline is in place, even if provisionally, you can begin assembling and categorizing your notes and ideas into these sections and organizing these into points to be made. From this basis, the writing itself can begin. Modularizing the work this way is one of the great benefits of having a structured outline, with sections (or modules). That outline itself may well be developed iteratively.

Against the background of these general considerations, I now have some specific tactical suggestions to add to those discussed in Section 4.7.

8.3 INSTITUTIONAL GUIDELINES

No matter how obvious it seems, an important tactical issue right at the start of proposal development is to find out what departmental and/or university guidelines, regulations and policies apply, both to the proposal and to the final dissertation. Locke et al. (2011) note that there will usually be three main sources of regulation: 'Normally, the planning and execution of student research are circumscribed by existing departmental policy on format for the final report, university regulations concerning thesis and dissertation reports, and informal standards exercised by individual advisors or study committees.'

They point out also that there is wide variation in specificity between departments and universities. Some regulations are very explicit ('the proposal may not exceed 25 type-written pages' or 'the proposal will conform to the style established in the *Publication Manual* of the American Psychological Association'), whereas others are very general ('the research topic must be of suitable proportions' or 'the proposal must reflect a thorough knowledge of the problem area').

As well as checking on departmental and/or university and/or dissertation committee regulations and guidelines regarding the proposal, it is useful also to find out about the process of proposal evaluation and approval in your department, and, if possible, to consult previous successful proposals. You can learn a lot from reading these, and it too usually makes your task seem less formidable.

Time and length guidelines might be laid down, and increasingly universities are placing size limits on proposals and dissertations. Two main reasons for this are that the sheer volume of research going on today demands some limit on the size of proposals (and dissertations), and that a strong argument can be made that it is good discipline to be able to describe the proposed research (or completed project) in a certain limited number of words or pages. According to this argument, it is important to develop the skill to say what you need to say about your research within these limits of time and length.

On the other hand, to give a full treatment of all the issues raised in this book (including, as appropriate, those in Chapter 5) may well require a proposal document which might exceed these limits. What to do in these cases? My advice for this situation is to prepare a full version, along the lines described here, and then to summarize it down to the required length. This shows the review committee that you have done a thorough job in proposal preparation (you can indicate in your shortened version that a full version is available, and perhaps also include parts of it as an appendix). But also, the full version of the proposal will be an important contribution to the final dissertation itself. After the proposal is approved and the research is carried out, you will have to report it in a dissertation. That dissertation is expected to be a full and detailed report of the research, though again, it will be expected to conform to size limits. Much of what is written in the full version of the proposal can be imported directly into the final dissertation.

8.4 GETTING STARTED

It is important to be clear about the formal requirements of both faculty and university for developing and submitting your research proposal. It is also important to learn about the process for evaluation and approval of your proposal. Sometimes these things can be learned through organized orientation experiences for beginning research students. At other times, the learning may have to be more heuristic, through your questioning and discussion with other students. When starting on your research journey in a university department, be sure to check also on what research training is provided, and on what research methods courses are available. Familiarize yourself also with the dissertation library, and if relevant, the proposal library.

8.4.1 Area, topic and research questions

Getting started in developing a proposal means either being able to identify a research area and topic, and moving towards general and specific questions within that topic, or knowing the specific research question(s) of interest, and being able to locate those first within more general questions, and then within a topic and area.

Many writers have discussed ways of getting started in research, and the sources and types of research areas and topics. Thus Locke et al. (2011) suggest that research questions emerge from three broad sources: logic, practicality and accident. As good practical advice for beginning research students, they also recommend the benefits of conversing with peers, listening to professorial discussions, assisting in research projects, attending lectures and conferences, exchanging papers and corresponding with faculty and students at other institutions. Neumann (1994: 110) suggests seven ways of selecting topics: personal experience, curiosity based on something in the media, the state of knowledge in a field, solving a problem (often associated with professional experience), 'social premiums', personal values and everyday life. Gitlin and Lyons (2008) discuss seven different sources of ideas for funding: clinical or professional experience, professional literature, interaction with others, societal trends, legislative initiatives, public documents, and agency goals and priorities.

In addition to the journal and dissertation literature, work experience and workplace issues and the media, experts or authorities – especially professional associations – will often make pronouncements about research needs. Consultancy work you might have been involved in is another possible source of research areas and topics, as are your previous studies. And in some areas – for example, business and management – trade sources will be useful.

Characteristics of good topics include access, achievable in time, value and suitable scope (Gill and Johnson, 2011). Two related don'ts to remember are:

- Don't pick a topic to solve a personal issue (Bryant, 2004: 18).
- Don't use your dissertation to 'grind an axe'.

8.4.2 Supervision and supervisors

Supervision is of central importance to the dissertation student and the dissertation experience, as is choosing a supervisor – assuming you have that choice. Factors to consider about prospective supervisors in making the choice include:

- *Area of research*. What research area(s) does this person work in, and how does that area relate to your proposed area? A perfect match is not necessary, but some intersection or overlap is desirable.
- *Methodological background and expertise*. What are the person's methodological preferences, and areas of expertise, especially on the central methodological issue for empirical research of quantitative, qualitative or mixed method? Important related questions are: do you know your own position on this, and the reasons for it? Is there compatibility between your methodological position and that of a prospective supervisor?
- *Supervision record*. Is there a track record of successful supervision? Departmental and university records will help here, as will consultations with other students. Sometimes tactful direct discussion of this is possible, but at other times more discreet and less obtrusive methods are better. Of course, this question needs to be de-emphasized if the staff member is very young, or has only recently begun academic work.
- *Supervision style* (especially with respect to flexibility and independence). This can usually only be determined by direct discussion with the supervisor, and by consulting other students with whom that supervisor has worked. Supervision styles can vary from very directive and prescriptive on the one hand, to very flexible and student-centred – aimed at encouraging independence – on the other. While on this topic, a good piece of general advice is not to become too dependent on your supervisor. Supervisors are generally not there to tell you what to do, and the university tradition for postgraduate dissertation work is one of 'independent study under supervision'.
- *Availability*. As academic workloads (often including travel) increase, availability becomes more and more important. There is no point in having an expert supervisor who is seldom available for consultation and feedback.
- *Approachability*. Initial contacts and discussions are important here, as are the experiences of other students. While approachability is desirable, Marshall and Green (2010) have a timely list of what your supervisor is not. Among other things, your supervisor is not 'your boss, your employer, your colleague, your best friend, your editor, your search engine, your wet-nurse'.

When approaching possible supervisors, it is useful to prepare by thinking about your motivations for doing a research degree, your proposed area of research, your methodological orientations and preferences (with reasons), and the type of relationship you believe you would prefer with a supervisor. In the PhD context, Marshall and Green (2010) have a helpful list of ten questions to ask prospective supervisors.

Once the choice of supervisor has been made, there is the question of managing the ongoing relationship. Relevant issues here include the frequency (and form) of meetings and discussions, supervisor expectations for the form and content of work to be submitted, and student expectations for the turnaround time and level of feedback for submitted work. These are best dealt with in direct discussion early in the supervision relationship.

Of course it is possible for things to go wrong, and how disagreements and disputes are handled becomes important. Most universities will have a code of supervisory practice, and it is important for the student to be aware of this. In extreme cases, the relationship may break down completely, or become dysfunctional. Change of supervision then becomes necessary.

8.4.3 The 'two-pager'

Often a good way to formalize getting started, after some period of work, is to write *no more than two pages* describing, as clearly and directly as possible, what the proposed research is trying to find out, and how it will do it. Students usually have some difficulty doing this. I find that common faults are for the one or two pages to expand to five, six or ten, and for the focus to be on the context, background and literature somehow relevant to the issue, rather than on the issue itself – the 'what' and the 'how' of the proposed research. These things, the context, background and literature, of course have their place. But the value of this exercise, at this point in the process, is in forcing a confrontation with the central questions of 'what am I trying to find out?' and 'how am I going to do it?', in that order. Limiting this document to two pages is a deliberate strategy to get past the context and background.

Like other stages in proposal development, getting satisfactory and stable answers to these questions is inevitably an iterative process. It takes several tries, and almost nobody gets it right the first time. In any case, the two-pager is a work-in-progress document. Its function is to see where your thinking is up to, so you can take it to the next stage. Its benefit is to get systematic thinking started, and to ensure an early focus on writing, with these central questions in mind.

As a supervisor, I most often find that discussing a first attempt at this two-pager with the student leads naturally to a second (and sometimes third and fourth) attempt, and that these attempts progressively produce a clearer initial statement. Once that is in place, even if tentatively, it provides the springboard for the next stage of thinking, reading and discussing. You can see what you need to do next.

8.4.4 The ideas paper

Another useful strategy – sometimes instead of the two-pager, sometimes alongside it – is to write an ideas paper, which sets out to sketch the context and background to the proposed topic, and which probably deals also with some of the main themes in the literature. A primary purpose here is to identify main issues, points or themes, with a view to proceeding more or less deductively from these to general and then to specific research questions. When progress is not deductive, but more interactive, moving backwards and forwards between general and specific issues, the ideas paper can have value in stimulating this. The trick is not to let it become the main focus of this stage of work, but to use it to lead into the central 'what' and 'how' questions.

What I call here an 'ideas paper' is sometimes called a 'preliminary discussion paper' or a 'discussion and concept paper' (Gilpatrick, 1989: 45, 101; Maxwell, 2012). These labels and interpretations are often valuable for the researcher who focuses on the problem rather than the question. Whatever they might be called, such papers will normally bring the benefits of helping you to sort out your ideas on a topic, indicating and perhaps starting to draw on relevant literature (what do others know or say about this topic?), and bringing into focus what you already know about the topic, perhaps from an experiential base.

8.4.5 Working deductively

If you are stuck, or are having trouble organizing your ideas and making them systematic, referring again to the hierarchy of concepts in Chapter 4 can help. From the most general to the most specific, that hierarchy is: research area, research topic, general research questions, specific research questions, data collection questions. We can develop from that hierarchy a simple set of deductive steps for developing a research proposal. Thus, for example, a six-step model is to:

- select a research area;
- develop one or more topics within that area;
- select one from among these topics to keep your project manageable;
- develop research questions, general and specific, for this topic;
- determine what data would be required to answer each specific research question;
- select research design, data collection and data analysis procedures in order to do this.

The value of this sort of thinking is not as a lock-step, formula-like approach to research planning. Rather, it is a useful 'fall-back' frame of reference for an overloaded or confused research planner. And you do not have to start this process from the top and work down. You can start from the middle – for example, with a particular specific research question of interest – and then move up and down the set of steps, up and down the hierarchy of concepts as appropriate.

8.5   THE VALUE OF DISCUSSION

Ultimately, in its written form, the proposal must go to some wider audience. At that stage, as noted earlier, the ideal completed proposal is a stand-alone document, able to be read and understood (and, in due course, approved) by a mixture of expert and non-expert readers. A valuable step, on the way to that, is discussing your developing ideas. Discussing is itself a process, in miniature, of taking your work to a wider audience.

Discussion with whom? In my opinion, with anybody you find helpful – but especially with your supervisor(s), with other research students and/or colleagues and/or others working in similar areas, and with non-expert friends, acquaintances and so on. This last type of discussant, being non-expert, might play the very valuable role of the 'naïve inquirer'. As Bryant (2004: 13) points out: "The more widely you converse about your topic, the clearer you will be about it." Such discussion includes brainstorming, which can help in topic identification and development.

Discussing your developing proposal has several benefits for your work:

- It is a step towards writing things down; both discussing your ideas with others and writing them down force you to think about structuring and representing your ideas so that they can be understood by others.
- It is a part of the clarification/communication process; you are required both to plan and to design a piece of research, and communicate that plan to others.
- It brings feedback from others, which is often important in clarification.
- It may suggest aspects of, or perspectives on, your topic that have so far escaped you.
- Discussion with experts may suggest literature you need to consult; discussion with non-experts may suggest aspects of the context or situation you need to take into account.

Always remember, however, despite the value of discussion, that the proposal must ultimately be a written document.

8.6   THE VALUE OF WRITING IT DOWN

'Like the turtle, we progress only with our necks stuck out.' This is often good advice on proposal development. Translated, it means: have a go at writing your ideas down, especially if you are stuck, or if you are at a point where you have done quite a lot of reading and thinking and it is time to try to capture, consolidate and perhaps order your ideas. You do this sort of writing 'as best as you can see things at the moment', knowing that this is a draft, a step on the way to a finished product. This exercise will throw up points and issues that need more thought, discussion or reading. But its main value is in clarifying your thinking. As with discussion, the structuring and representation of ideas are involved here, as is the relationship between thinking and writing. The main value here of the concrete activity of writing it down, for someone else to read, is in clarification. This is an example of 'writing to learn' or writing to discover. More accurately, it is an example of writing in order to sort things out. It is useful to regularize and formalize such writing into a research journal, which continues during the dissertation.

8.7 THREE COMMON DILEMMAS

This section deals with three dilemmas which often occur as students develop proposals. The first is the problem of several topics at once; the second is focusing on the context, background and literature versus focusing on the research questions; and the third is getting to closure versus getting to closure too quickly. I think of these as tensions in the research planning process, which are almost inevitable as work on the proposal progresses.

8.7.1 Several topics at once

One common problem students experience is selecting a research area and topic, and getting the development of the proposal started. But another common problem is finding that there is more than one topic (or proposal, or project) emerging, as the student continues to work. There are two main versions of this problem. One is deciding among possible research areas and topics. The other is deciding among possible research questions, after the area and topic have been selected.

A situation frequently encountered is where the student can see more than one, and perhaps several, attractive research areas and questions. These may be related to each other, or they may be rather unconnected and discrete. This situation is most common early in the process of developing the proposal. As Brink and Wood (1994: xii) say: 'Perhaps the hardest task of all is deciding on one well-defined topic. There is so much to do that it is hard not to want to do it all at once.'

Faced with this problem, one strategy to consider is to develop more than one idea, as a possible proposal, up to a certain point. Most of the time, none of us can see clearly, up-front and in advance of a certain amount of work, where any one topic or set of questions might lead. Therefore, instead of trying to make judgements too early, it is better to push ahead with more than one topic for a period of time, in order to see where each leads: what type of study each leads to, how feasible and 'doable' each is, how each fits with the interests, preferences and situation of the student, and so on.

The two-pager is helpful here. Of course there comes a time when judgements are needed as to future directions, and decisions have to be made. The point here is that keeping the options open for a time, while more than one area is explored, is often good policy.

The second aspect of this problem is when we discover, through the question development stage, that an initial apparently quite straightforward topic has much more in it that first meets the eye. This is by no means uncommon, and we usually only get to see this by developing the topic and its questions to a reasonable extent.

What generally happens after a period of question development (see Section 4.7.1) is that the project has expanded, sometimes greatly. This can cause anxiety, but for most projects it should happen. In fact, if it does not, we should probably be concerned, since it may be a sign of insufficient question development work. Therefore, it is to be encouraged, within reason, as an important stage. Probing, exploring, and seeing other possibilities with a topic can be valuable before reaching closure on the specific directions for a project.

When a small set of starting questions has multiplied into a larger set, disentangling and ordering are required. Disentangling is necessary because one question will often have other questions within it. Ordering involves categorizing, and the grouping of questions together. This will soon become hierarchical, and general and specific research questions begin to be distinguishable from each other.

The final stage then involves bringing the project down to size, since it has usually become too big. In fact, it probably suggests a research programme with several research projects by now. How is this trimming done? It involves deciding which questions are manageable within the practical constraints of this project, and which seem the most central and important. There are of course limits around any project – even if that project involves a substantial grant and a team of researchers. The principle here is that it is better to do a smaller project thoroughly than a larger project superficially. Trimming a project down to size is a matter of judgement, and experience in research has a big role to play here. Once again, therefore, this stage is best done in collaboration with others. This stage is sometimes called delimiting the project. This means drawing the boundaries around it, and showing what is not in the project, as well as what is.

How many research questions should there be? There are practical limitations on any one project, and, as noted, it is better to have a small job done thoroughly than a large job done only superficially. More than about three or four general research questions, assuming that each is subdivided into (say) two or three specific questions, is testing the upper limit of what can be done in one study.

8.7.2   Getting to closure versus getting to closure too quickly

Many higher-degree programmes combine course work and a research dissertation. Completing the coursework is not normally the problem for most higher-degree students. Completing the dissertation sometimes is. The first major step in completing the dissertation is to complete the research proposal and have it accepted.

For some students, the process of choosing a research area and topic, pondering its complexities, mastering its literature, and formulating questions and methods to guide the investigation can take too long. Indeed, as with the dissertation itself, there is usually a time limit imposed on this stage of the work. This reflects the view, noted earlier, that part of the task is to get the job (proposal or dissertation) done within a certain period of time, and to get the story told within a certain number of words.

This means that there is a point at which, after an appropriate period of time, consideration and work, it is necessary to make decisions and complete the proposal. It is necessary to 'get to closure'. It helps in doing this to remember the following:

- There is no such thing as a perfect research proposal (or dissertation) – all research can be criticized.
- It is appropriate to be aware of, and to make the reader aware of, difficulties, problems and limitations, while not being overly defensive about the research.
- Not all of the issues which might arise in a piece of research have to be dealt with in the proposal. Some might well be dealt with after acceptance of the proposal, in the execution stage of the research itself. In these cases, they should be noted in the proposal.
- Emergent and unfolding designs will naturally be less definitive at the proposal stage than those which take a highly preplanned and prestructured approach.

However, while some students have trouble getting to closure, there is also the opposite problem of getting to closure too quickly. That is why the phrase 'after an appropriate period of time' was used above. During this planning stage, there is some benefit to hastening slowly. Since research questions do not usually come out right the first time, several iterations are often required, and we only reach a full answer to the question 'What are we trying to find out?' after careful thought. This question development stage needs time – time to see the possible questions buried in an area and to see related questions which follow from an analysis of particular questions. The theme in Section 4.7.1 was the importance of the pre-empirical, setting-up stage of the research – the decisions taken here will influence what is done in later stages. This does not mean that the decisions cannot be varied, as when iteration towards the final research questions goes on during the early empirical stages of the project. But varying them should not be done lightly if considerable effort has been invested in reaching them during the setting-up stage.

8.7.3 Focus on context, background and literature versus focus on research questions

Clearly, both context, background and literature on the one hand, and research questions on the other, are necessary in the finished proposal (or dissertation). So it is not a question of one of these things or the other. The issue here is about the focus on each, and especially about the timing of the focus on each, in developing the proposal.

On the one hand, focusing too much on the context, background and the literature too early in the process of research planning can result in lengthy essays on these topics, delaying (sometimes almost indefinitely) the proposal itself. It can also strongly affect the direction of the research, not always beneficially. On the other hand, focusing only on the research questions runs the risk of unnecessary, uninformed and inappropriate duplication of research, and of decontextualizing the research.

The solution, as usual, is a matter of judgement, in how the two things are balanced and integrated. Some of both is essential, and no formula can be prescribed for general use. With some topics, approaches and students, it is appropriate to focus heavily on research questions and methods until major directions for the research have been set. With others, it is important to get the context, background and literature integrated into the thinking early.

At the same time, I often feel that the danger of a student being overwhelmed by, or at least strongly influenced by, the literature especially, and to a lesser extent being preoccupied with matters of context and background, can be worse than the danger of developing research questions in isolation from literature, context and background. I think this is especially true in applied social science areas, where the student often brings important knowledge to the research. I do not believe that knowledge should be ignored.

That is why I usually recommend focusing, firstly, on the 'what' and 'how' of the research, and then fitting context, background and literature around that. But overall the process is interactive. And, for most proposals, the writer moves backwards and forwards between the context–background–literature and the research questions, as the proposal develops.

8.8 THE IMPORTANCE OF CLARITY

Finally, and as noted several times already, your proposal will be much more convincing if it is clear. Recapping what has been said about academic writing in Section 7.4, two main ideas are involved in achieving this:

- *Organizing for understanding*. The proposal will be easier for readers to understand, especially in the stand-alone context described, if it is structured in a logical and coherent way. This means there should be clearly identified sections, which together cover the material expected, and which are suitably interconnected with each other. It also means that, as a writer, you are putting yourself in the position of the reader, and anticipating reader reactions.
- *Writing for clarity*. Writing for the academic research context demands both acceptable scholarly format, and clarity. Both, and especially the latter, take time. Good writing, in this context, is invariably the result of drafting and redrafting, sharpening and shortening.

I agree with Locke et al. (2011) when they suggest the need for 'semantic and conceptual hygiene'. Your thinking in a research situation needs to be systematic, organized and disciplined. Your writing needs to reflect that. Semantic and conceptual hygiene should lead on to linguistic hygiene.

8.9 REVIEW CONCEPTS

Proposal guidelines   Universities and departments typically have their own guidelines and requirements for proposals. It is important to follow these.

Proposal approval   Universities and departments typically also have established procedures for proposal consideration and approval. Again, it is important to be aware of these.

Supervisor(s)   Supervision is an important component of higher-degree research programmes, and this chapter gives guidelines for choice of supervisor (if appropriate).

The 'two-pager'   A brief outline of the area and topic, purpose, research questions and proposed methods; deliberately ignores background, context and literature in order to get proposal development moving.

The 'ideas paper'   A longer document which draws on background, context and literature as appropriate to identify main themes and ideas which lead to the proposed research and its purpose(s).

Organizing for understanding   Structuring the proposal logically, with sections and subsections, to facilitate a reader's understanding.

Writing for clarity   Academic research writing relies heavily on clarity, and needs to be presented in acceptable scholarly format.

───────── EXERCISES AND STUDY QUESTIONS ─────────

1. Locate and read the institutional guidelines for research proposals which are relevant to your situation. If you are studying in a university, there may be two sets of these – a university-wide set and a departmental set.
2. Find out the process for proposal approval which applies in your situation.
3. Write a 'two-pager', as described in earlier in this chapter.
4. Write a short 'ideas paper' (3–5 pages), as described earlier in this chapter. This can later feed into the introduction to your proposal.
5. Identify one or more possible supervisors for your project. If possible and appropriate, discuss your research ideas with them. (Your 'two-pager' will be helpful here).
6. Identify which body of literature is relevant to your research (there may be more than one). Indicate how you will deal with the literature in your proposal (see Chapter 5, p. 72 for the three general possibilities).

9

EXAMPLES OF PROPOSALS

This chapter includes five examples of proposals – two quantitative, two qualitative and one mixed-method. Two are from educational research and the other three are from social medicine, management/business and nursing. A caveat is now required. I have tried to write this as a general book for developing social science research proposals, without wishing to favour one style or type or approach over others. Since space reasons make it impossible to have proposals for all different types of research in this one book, any selection runs the risk of appearing to favour one sort of research over another, or of suggesting a 'template' for students to follow (Maxwell, 2012). That is not intended. Rather, the five proposals are included as examples of best practice, and they are included here without comment. They illustrate many of the points made in earlier chapters.

I have retained the sections and section headings of the original proposals, rather than trying to standardize them into a common set of headings. Different universities, and sometimes different departments within the one university, vary in proposal format requirements. At the same time, each proposal included here meets – in one way or another – the reader's expectations described in Section 2.2 and covered in the general set of headings given in Table 7.1. At doctoral level, universities often ask candidates in their proposal to address the way in which the proposed research will meet the doctoral criterion of a 'substantial and original contribution to knowledge', and that section is included here, where it applies. Other proposal headings – such as timetable, estimated costs, appendices and research instruments – which are less relevant to this book are omitted from the versions of the proposal shown here, as are details of references, for space reasons.

Aside from these omissions, the five proposals are presented in full. They are followed in Section 9.6 by a list of examples of some other proposals in the literature. This list gives an idea of the range and diversity of proposals, with titles included where available to indicate the area and topic of the research.

9.1 QUANTITATIVE PROPOSAL: EDUCATION

Name of candidate: *Nola Purdie*

Degree: Doctor of Philosophy, The University of Western Australia

A. Proposed study

(i) Title

A cross-cultural investigation of the relationship between student conceptions of learning and their use of self-regulated learning strategies.

(ii) Aims

For a variety of reasons there is an increasing number of overseas students, particularly from South-East Asian countries, who are being educated in Australian schools. Differences in schooling and cultural traditions lead to different understandings of what learning actually is and to the strategies students use to regulate their own learning. Although it is not possible to speak with accuracy of an 'Asian' culture, it is, nevertheless, possible to identify several cultural characteristics that strongly influence understandings and practices related to education and learning that appear to be common across a number of Asian countries (Biggs, 1991; Garner, 1991; Hess and Azume, 1991; Thomas, 1990). In particular, concepts of filial piety and self-control, and an emphasis on rote memorization as a way of learning, contrast strongly with the qualities of independence of thought, verbal assertiveness, and learning through the development of meaning which are promoted as desirable behaviours in Australian students. If Australian teachers are to cater successfully for students from other cultures, it is important that we develop a better understanding of what these students actually think learning is and how they go about doing it.

This research, therefore, aims to determine if cultural differences in understandings about the nature of learning and the strategies used by students to perform a range of academic tasks do exist. Specifically, the research will compare the conceptions of learning and the use of self-regulated learning strategies of Australian secondary school students for whom English is a first language with those of students from two different South-East Asian countries (hereafter referred to collectively as Asian students). The research will test the hypothesis that what students understand by learning will, to a certain extent, determine their use of self-regulated learning strategies.

It is expected that the experience of schooling in Australia will cause changes in understandings about the nature of learning and the use of learning strategies. To investigate these changes, comparisons will be made between Asian students before they have been exposed to schooling in Australia and Asian students who have had several years of education in Australia and for whom English is a second language. The relationship between the level of English language proficiency of the Asian students and their use of self-regulated learning strategies will also be explored.

(iii) Substantial contribution to knowledge

The proposed research represents a substantial and original contribution to knowledge in that a cross-cultural perspective will be taken with respect to the investigation of students' conceptions of learning and their use of learning strategies. The research project will extend and integrate theory and findings from several areas of research relating to student learning. Self-regulated learning theory, developed through research from Western participants, will be applied to participants from two different South-East Asian countries. The motivational component of self-regulated learning will be explored with a view to expanding the already established output notion of what prompts students to engage in self-regulated learning to include an input component. Finally, theory that suggests that second language competence may be a factor in student use of self-regulated learning strategies will be tested.

(iv) Theoretical framework

Introduction

The importance of self-regulation in learning has now been firmly established (Bandura, 1989; Zimmerman, 1990b). In contrast to investigations of student achievement that focus on student ability as the key factor in learning, self-regulation theory focuses attention on *why* and *how* students become initiators and controllers of their own learning. *How* students self-regulate has largely been explained by the degree to which a student is aware of and uses appropriately specific strategies to achieve their academic goals. The *why* of self-regulation has been explained in terms of motivational processes that are dependent on learning outcomes which have either tangible or intangible personal implications. 'Behaviorally oriented approaches focus on tangible outcomes such as material or social gains, whereas cognitively oriented approaches emphasize intangible outcomes such as self-actualization, self-efficacy, or reduced cognitive dissonance' (Zimmerman, 1990: 11).

The proposed research seeks to extend this view of motivational causation to include another component. In current theory, outcomes, both tangible and intangible, are considered to be the prime motivators of self-regulation in learning. A theory will be developed that posits inputs as an important, additional motivational factor. Specifically, input is that which students bring to academic tasks thereby prompting them to be proactive and systematic controllers of the learning process. In contrast to outcomes, where the focus is on a future-oriented actuality, inputs are derived from past experiences and are very much active in the present. Although there are bound to be several different sources of inputs, this research will focus on just one – student conceptions of learning. It will be argued, and subsequently tested, that what students understand by learning will, to a certain extent, determine their use of self-regulated strategies.

Self-regulated learning

Many studies have established the relationship between achievement, strategy use, and verbal self-efficacy in self-regulated learning (e.g. Bandura, 1982; Schunk, 1984; Zimmerman and Martinez-Pons, 1986, 1990) but this research has used Western participants for whom English is their first language. There are two potential problems with generalizing from these studies to second language users from a non-Western background. First, there may not be cross-cultural conceptual equivalence regarding the notion of self-regulated learning; and second, competence in the use of English may influence a student's ability to use self-regulated strategies, particularly those which are, in part, dependent on the four macro language skills of speaking, listening, reading and writing.

Self-regulation theory evolved out of an understanding of self-control as the product of socialization processes aimed at the development of moral standards of conduct (Bandura, 1977). Zimmerman (1990) noted Bandura's later extension of this theory to include a goal related aspect. A person's goals and expectations are seen to provide the motivational stimulus to the self-control of behaviour which is directed at effecting changes in self or situation.

One current theory of self-regulated learning perceives students to be self-regulated learners to the extent that they are metacognitively, motivationally and behaviourally active participants in their own learning processes (Zimmerman, 1986). This theory proposes that self-regulated learning involves three key elements: use of self-regulated learning strategies, self-efficacy perceptions of performance skill, and commitment to academic goals (Zimmerman, 1990). Self-regulated learning strategies involve agency, purpose and instrumentality self-perceptions by a learner and are aimed at acquiring information and skill. Furthermore, this theory proposes triad reciprocal causality among three influence processes: personal, behavioural, and environmental (Bandura, 1986; Zimmerman, 1989).

Based on this view of self-regulated learning, a structured interview for assessing student use of self-regulated learning strategies was developed (Zimmerman and Martinez-Pons, 1986). The Self-Regulated Learning Interview Schedule (SRLIS) has been used to correlate student strategy use with academic achievement (Zimmerman and Martinez-Pons, 1986); with teacher ratings of students' use of self-regulatory strategies, and students' verbal achievement (Zimmerman and Martinez-Pons, 1988); and with student perceptions of both verbal and mathematical efficacy (Zimmerman and Martinez-Pons, 1990). It is planned to use a form of the SRLIS, modified to cater for cross-cultural differences in educational context, to assess the strategy use of subjects in the proposed research project.

Conceptions of learning

Students' conceptions of learning have been found to be one component of the skill of self-regulated learning (Säljö, 1979). According to Säljö, when students perceive learning to be a reproductive process, the responsibility for transmitting an already existing body of knowledge into the head of the learner lies with an external source. In contrast, however, when learning is viewed as a meaning-centred process, the learner is more likely to assume responsibility for construing knowledge by proactively initiating and regulating the (re)construction process.

Six distinctly different conceptions of learning have been identified in research (Marton, Dall'Alba and Beatty, 1993; Säljö, 1979). These six different conceptions (increasing one's knowledge, memorizing and reproducing, applying, understanding, seeing something in a different way, and changing as a person) have been used in research to demonstrate that students from different cultures do conceive of learning in different ways (Marton, 1992; Watkins and Regmi, 1992). There are two aspects to a person's conception of learning: a way of seeing *what* is learned and a way of seeing *how* it is learned (Marton, Dall'Alba and Beatty, 1993). The implications for self-regulation learning theory with regard to the *how* of learning are clear. *How* a student perceives learning to occur will determine the set of strategies selected to achieve the desired outcome.

There is some evidence to suggest that students from different cultures do understand learning in different ways (Watkins and Regmi, 1992). If this is so for students from South-East Asian countries who are being schooled in Australia, then there are obvious implications for teachers and the classroom practices adopted by them.

Second language competence and self-regulated learning

Research findings that verbal achievement and verbal efficacy are correlated significantly with strategy use (Zimmerman and Martinez-Pons, 1988, 1990) are particularly pertinent to this proposed study. It is hypothesized that second language users, who are not yet fully competent in their second language, will be disadvantaged in their use of self-regulated strategies because of assumed weaknesses in verbal ability and verbal efficacy. Of the 14 strategies identified by Zimmerman and Martinez-Pons (1986), half (self-evaluation, organizing and transforming, seeking information, keeping records and monitoring, rehearsing and memorizing, seeking social assistance – from peers, teachers, and adults, reviewing records – tests, notes and textbooks) require students to use one or more of the macro skills of speaking, listening, reading and writing in the target language. Depending on the level of development in these four skills, students will be variously disadvantaged in their attempts to employ strategies that require direct use of one or more of the macro skills in their second language.

The interaction between language proficiency and the use of self-regulated strategies is further complicated by the verbalizations or private speech of students. Such speech is directed towards the self in order to facilitate the execution of a task. It has been shown to improve coding, storage, and retention of information thereby aiding the process of future retrieval and use (Denney, 1975; Schunk, 1986); verbalization can improve students' self-efficacy for performing tasks (Schunk, 1986) which in turn can promote task motivation and learning (Schunk, 1985); by using self-reinforcement and coping with verbalizations, students may be better able to maintain a positive task orientation and cope with difficulties (Michenbaum and Asarnow, 1979). These findings all point to the key role of verbalization in developing self-regulated learning in students.

Another potential problem for second language users lies in the area of the use of the social strategies of self-regulated learning (i.e. seeking assistance from peers, teachers, and other adults). In this respect, not only is there the problem of limited oral proficiency which could well discourage students from attempting to use these strategies but there is also the possibility of conflict arising out of different cultural and educational backgrounds. For some second language users, it is perceived to be inappropriate behaviour to seek personal assistance from the teacher. Furthermore, even though the seeking of assistance from peers may be viewed as acceptable behaviour by second language users, and is a previously highly practised activity for some (Tang, 1990), lack of confidence in their ability to approach peers successfully, to be clearly understood and to correctly understand their responses may be too strong a deterrent to the use of this strategy.

Finally, there is some research that suggests that studying in a second language will influence a student's approach to learning (Watkins, Biggs and Regmi, 1991). Students less confident in a second language tend to rely more on rote learning whereas those with greater confidence are low on surface and high on deep approaches to learning. This suggests that an increase in second language competence will be associated with an increased ability to employ self-regulated learning strategies in the execution of academic tasks.

(v) Research questions

1. What self-regulated learning strategies are used by Asian students in their native educational settings?
2. Do the self-regulated learning strategies of Asian students change when they become learners in Australian schools, using English as a second language? If so, in what ways?
3. What do Asian students actually understand by the term 'learning'?
4. Do the conceptions of learning held by Asian students change when they become students in Australian schools?
5. What is the relationship between students' conceptions of learning and their use of self-regulated strategies?
6. What, if any, are the differences between the conceptions of learning and the use of self-regulated learning strategies of Asian and Australian students?
7. Does the level of English language competence of Asian students in Australian schools affect their use of self-regulated learning strategies?

B. Research plan
(i) Methods and approaches
Study 1

Purpose   The purpose of this study is to design an interview schedule that is appropriate for use with both Australian secondary school students and students from two different Asian countries. In order for an interview schedule to provide reliable and valid information, a number of factors need to be kept in mind. Segall (1986) noted the following as important considerations in the construction of a cross-cultural interview schedule: efficiency with relation to time and cost; the construction of a set of questions which serve a purpose, which are unambiguous, which allow the interviewer to insert probe questions to obtain more elaboration of answers already given, and which make it easy for the respondent to answer; the use of translation techniques that will maximize correct interpretation of responses; and the development of appropriate coding and scoring systems.

Using the above guidelines for the construction of a reliable and valid instrument, an interview schedule, based on that developed by Zimmerman and Martinez-Pons (1986, 1990), will be designed. This interview schedule will assess the different categories of self-regulated learning strategies (self-evaluation; organizing and transforming; goal-setting and planning; seeking information; keeping records and monitoring; environmental structuring; self-consequences; rehearsing and memorizing; seeking peer, teacher or adult assistance; reviewing tests, notes, and texts; and other).

A number of different learning contexts will be identified both from the Zimmerman and Martinez-Pons studies and from pilot interviews with newly arrived Asian students and students who are accustomed to the Australian secondary school learning environment. This will ensure that learning contexts will be valid for all participants taking part in this research. The following is an example of a learning context that could be described:

> Imagine your teacher is discussing with your class the influence of twentieth-century developments in technology on the lives of people today. Your teacher says that you will be tested on the topic the next day. Do you have a method that you would use to help you learn and remember the information being discussed? What if you are having trouble understanding or remembering the information discussed in class?

> (adapted from Zimmerman and Martinez-Pons, 1990)

Zimmerman and Martinez-Pons (1986) described procedures for the coding of protocols which resulted in an interrater agreement level of 86%. Three different scoring procedures – strategy use, strategy frequency and strategy consistency – were developed to summarize the categorical data obtained. A pilot study using a small group of students from Perth metropolitan schools will be used to check the appropriateness of these procedures and refine them where possible. This group of students will include representatives of the three types of students used for this research and who are described in the following two studies.

Study 2

Purpose   This study will investigate conceptions of learning and the use of self-regulated strategies of Asian students from two different countries before they have been exposed to schooling in Australia.

Participants   The participants will be 60 newly arrived Asian students who are about to commence an intensive English language programme prior to entry into upper secondary (Years 11 and 12) education in Perth. Costs associated with the translation of interview data make it impossible to include students from a large number of Asian countries. Students from two Asian countries will be selected from Perth schools, depending on availability at the time of the study. In order to ensure that responses to questions in the interview schedule are based on the learning strategies students have developed for use in their native learning environments rather than strategies that have been influenced by exposure to other learning environments, it is important that students have not had previous schooling in a non-native learning environment.

Procedures   The self-regulated learning interview schedule developed in Study 1 will be presented separately to each student in his or her native language by trained interviewers. The interviewers will have been acquainted with the nature and purpose of the study and trained to present the interview schedule in such a way as to elicit from students answers that are as fully elaborated as possible. A number of different learning contexts will be described to students and they will be asked to indicate the methods they would normally use in the situations described.

Students will also be asked to respond to the question 'What do you actually understand by learning?'

Student responses to questions will be recorded by the interviewer who will later translate these into English. All interviews will be tape-recorded to enable subsequent checking of responses.

Data analysis   Coding and scoring procedures developed in Study 1 will be applied to student responses to the self-regulated learning interview schedule.

Using methodology described by Marton and Säljö (1984), responses to the question about conceptions of learning will be analysed and coded according to the six levels: increasing one's knowledge; memorizing and reproducing; applying; understanding; seeing something in a different way; and changing as a person. Briefly, this approach to the analysis of the transcripts will involve the identification and grouping, on the basis of similarities, differences and complementarities, students' responses to the question 'What do you actually understand by learning?'

Multiple regression analyses will be used to determine if there is an association between learning strategy use and conceptions of learning. For instance, do students who use more self-regulated learning strategies tend to understand learning more in the last three ways as opposed to the first three ways?

Study 3

Purpose   The purpose of this study is to investigate the use of self-regulated strategies by two groups of secondary school students: native speakers of English; and Asian students whose second language is English, who have been studying in Australian schools for at least two years, and who have achieved at least an intermediate level of competence in the use of English. Patterns of strategy use of these two groups and the group of students from the second study will be compared in order to establish if differences exist between the groups.

The study will also investigate the conceptions of learning held by the native speakers of English and the Asian students. These will be compared with the conceptions of students in the first study.

Finally, the study will investigate the relationship between the two levels of English language proficiency (intermediate and advanced) and the patterns of self-regulated learning strategy use of the Asian students.

Participants   Ninety Year 12 students studying at Perth metropolitan high schools will be used for this study. Thirty will be native speakers of English and 60 will be non-native English speakers from similar Asian language backgrounds to those in the second study. They will have been studying in Australian schools for at least two years. Half of the non-English speaking background students will be at an 'intermediate' level of language proficiency and half will be at an 'advanced' level. Students will be assigned to proficiency groups according to language test scores and on teacher recommendation.

Procedure   The question 'What exactly do you understand by learning?' and the self-regulated learning interview schedule will be presented (in English) to students in a similar manner to that used in Study 2. Depending on information gained from Study 2 with respect to the category 'other', further categories of strategy will be added , or, if no new strategies did emerge, this category will remain as 'other'.

Data analysis   Responses to the strategy interview schedule and the question about conceptions of learning will be coded and scored as for Study 2. As the data will be frequency counts, log linear analysis will be used to assess differences in strategy use and conceptions of learning across the four groups.

(ii) What efforts have been made to ensure that the project does not duplicate work already done?

An extensive search of the literature has been undertaken since February, 1993. Searches on ERIC and Psychlit, and an examination of recent editions of CIJE and bibliographies obtained from key journal articles, have produced a large collection of readings related to self-regulated learning and conceptions of learning. Although these two areas have been well researched, a cross-cultural perspective has not been applied. Furthermore, the two areas have been researched independently of each other and no evidence of linking theory and findings in the manner proposed in this research has been found.

(iii) Confidentiality

All information pertaining to participants will remain the property of the researcher and will not be used for any purpose except for execution of this study. Students' names will not be used other than for organization of the raw data.

9.2 QUALITATIVE PROPOSAL: EDUCATION

Name of candidate: *Ron Chalmers*

Degree: Doctor of Philosophy, The University of Western Australia

A. Proposed study

(i) Title

The inclusion of children with a severe or profound intellectual disability in regular classrooms: how teachers manage the situation.

(ii) The research aim

The aim of this study is to use grounded theory methods to develop a theory about how primary school teachers in rural schools in Western Australia manage the situation of having a child with a severe or profound intellectual disability included in their classroom during the course of one school year.

Currently, in Western Australia, children with intellectual disabilities are taught in a variety of educational settings by teachers from a wide range of backgrounds. The vast majority of children with a severe or profound intellectual disability attend education support schools, centres or units. In rural and remote areas of the state where education support facilities do not exist, a relatively small number of children with this level of disability (35 primary school students in 1994) attend their local school and are included in a regular classroom. This study will focus on regular classroom teachers in country schools who are called upon to include a child with a severe or profound intellectual disability in their class.

The study will be limited to primary school teachers because, unlike their secondary school colleagues, they have the responsibility for the total educational programme and the duty of care for their class of students throughout the school day. Inclusion in secondary schools typically involves numerous teachers and a variety of classroom settings. Furthermore, the number of children with a severe or profound intellectual disability that are currently included in the regular classrooms of secondary schools is extremely small.

The study will use the criteria set by the Education Department of Western Australia to define severe and profound intellectual disability. The Department, utilizing the criteria for determining levels of severity developed by the Australian Council of Education Research, estimates that 0.1% of the population have a severe disability, and 0.05% of the population have a profound disability. A severely disabled child is described as having 'an IQ in the range 25 to 39, minimal speech and poor motor development, an inability to learn functional academic skills, and a capacity to profit from systematic habit-training' (de Lemos, 1993: 22). A profoundly disabled child is described as having 'an IQ below 24, minimal capacity for functioning, some motor or speech development, and a requirement of complete care and supervision' (de Lemos, 1993: 22).

In this proposal, the terms inclusive education and inclusion will be used deliberately in preference to the term integration. Inclusion will refer to situations in which a student with a disability is 'embedded within the normative educative pathways within the classroom and school' (Uditsky, 1993: 88), and in which the regular classroom teacher is responsible for the student's education. In contrast, in the Western Australia education system, the term integration is used to describe situations in which children with disabilities are located in education support units or centres, are the responsibility of education support teachers, and spend only parts of the school day in regular classrooms. In the wider education community the term integration has been used to describe many different types of placement. Terms such as physical integration, systematic integration, reciprocal integration, and associative integration are used to describe particular strategies for increasing the level of interaction between children with disabilities and their non-disabled peers. Each one of these forms of integration is something other than inclusive education as defined for this study.

(iii) The research context

The move towards the integration and inclusion of children with intellectual disabilities into mainstream education has been a feature of Western education systems for the past 15 years. This development has been largely the result of 'intensive advocacy for integration of people with disabilities into all areas of community life' (Sobsey and Dreimanis, 1993: 1).

Integrated or inclusive education contrasts markedly with the response of Western societies to the education of children with disabilities in earlier decades. At the turn of the last century the vast majority of children with intellectual disabilities were considered ineducable and subsequently excluded from any form of formal education (Galloway, 1985; Uditsky, 1993). In many countries there was no distinction made between children with intellectual disabilities and people with mental disorders. At the end of World War II, special education became a feature of public education in many countries (Barton and Tomlinson, 1986; Booth, 1981). Children with disabilities began to gain access to formal education, but only within the confines of special education systems.

The pressure for inclusion has come primarily from the parents of children with disabilities, educators and other community advocates (National Institute on Mental Retardation, 1981; Stainback, Stainback and Bunch, 1989). These groups have used powerful moral, social and political arguments in support of their case. One of the most persuasive arguments is that all children gain through inclusion. Studies indicate that, given proper guidance, students can learn in inclusive settings to understand, respect, be sensitive to, and grow comfortable with the individual differences and similarities amongst their peers (McHale and Simeonsson, 1980; Voeltz, 1980: 182). Stainback and Stainback (1985) observe that:

> there are many nonhandicapped persons who realise a tremendous range of emotional and social benefits from their involvements with persons who experience severe handicaps.

Advocates for inclusion also contend that segregated education leads to segregation in adult life, and that inclusion in education has the opposite effect. The assertion here is that positive attitudes toward people with disabilities are developed when disabled and non-disabled children interact at school, and that these attitudes are sustained in adult life (see, for example, Bricker, 1978; Snyder, Apolloni and Cooke, 1977).

Inclusion in education has also been portrayed as a human rights issue. The arguments used to enhance the participation rates of racial minorities and females in education have been used as the basis for promoting the inclusion of children with disabilities in schools. The landmark Victorian Report of the Ministerial Review of Educational Services for the Disabled (Collins, 1984) proposed that the development of policy be underpinned by five guiding principles. Significantly, the first principle was that every child has a right to be educated in an ordinary classroom in a regular class.

A number of commentators, including Biklen (1985) and Keogh (1990), have observed that the strength of the inclusive education movement has come from the values that underpin the cause rather than from the findings of studies into the outcomes of inclusion. According to Conway (1991), the introduction of policies intended to encourage inclusion has occurred not as an outcome of empirical research but as a result of changes in public attitudes about the way the wider community responds to people with disabilities.

It should not be inferred from this that there has been a dearth of research into aspects of inclusive education. The research literature in this field of education is extensive. The vast majority of this research has been characterized by the application of traditional quantitative methodologies. Experiments and questionnaire surveys in large-N studies have been the norm. The findings from quantitative research conducted during the past 15 years have contributed significantly to the field of special education and, more specifically, to the segregation–inclusion debate. Curriculum design, resourcing teacher training, administrative arrangements and efficacy research have been favoured areas for investigation.

There are, however, increasing calls for more qualitative research in this field of education (Biklen and Moeley, 1988; Hegarty and Evans, 1989; Patton, 1990; Salisbury, Palombaro and Hollowood, 1993; Stainback and Stainback, 1989). Hegarty (1989: 110) stated that there are 'many topics in special education that are best explored by means of qualitative methods of inquiry'. These include investigations into pupils' and teachers' perspectives and experiences of particular education programmes; clarifying the implications of various policy options; evaluating innovations; and providing detailed accounts of various forms of special education provision.

Despite these calls, Vulliamy and Webb (1993: 190) observed that:

> There have been relatively few published qualitative research studies on the theme of special education, despite the prominent impact of qualitative research on educational research more generally.

More research of this kind is needed to gain a greater understanding of the phenomenon of inclusive education from the perspectives of the people involved (teachers, parents, school administrators and students) in their natural settings. We need 'in-depth, penetrating investigation that strives for relational understanding of all the various factors that comprise and affect the object of the … study' (Wolf, 1979: 5). The development of theories about inclusion, grounded in data gathered from teachers and other school-based personnel, contribute significantly to this field of education, inform teachers who find themselves in similar situations in the future, and guide the development of policy for the education of students with disabilities.

There are clear indications that an increasing number of Australian children with intellectual disabilities will be educated in regular classrooms (see DEET, 1993; Education Department of Western Australia, 1992) and, correspondingly, that an increasing number of Western Australian primary school teachers will experience the phenomenon of inclusive education. Given that the outcomes of inclusion initiatives depend on the beliefs, values and attitudes of teachers (Cohen and Cohen, 1986), in the Western Australian context there needs to be a greater understanding of what teachers think and believe about this phenomenon, and how these thoughts and beliefs change over time.

(iv) This study's substantial and original contribution to knowledge

The aim of this study is to use grounded theory methods to build theory about a specific aspect of education where no theory currently exists. To date there is very little knowledge and no explanatory theory about the way primary school teachers in rural and remote schools manage inclusion. An extensive search of the research literature has failed to identify studies that have examined this particular phenomenon. The theory that will be generated from this study will be an original contribution to the knowledge base of the emerging field of inclusive education.

The importance of inclusive education in the 1990s

A number of recent developments indicate that the education of students with disabilities is one of the most important issues facing the Western Australian school system. In December 1992 the then Ministry of Education established the Task Force on the Education of Students with Disabilities and Specific Learning Difficulties in response to 'growing parent concerns about the problems faced by children with disabilities' (Ministerial Task Force, 1993: v). The Task Force report listed 60 recommendations to government. Many of these recommendations relate specifically to the role of the teacher in educating students with disabilities. In February 1994 the Minister for Education responded to the report. The Minister announced that the education of students with disabilities and specific learning difficulties would be a priority for the next three years and that schools will be required to reflect this in their school development plans. Additional resources ($6 million over the next triennium) will be allocated to implement recommendations in the Task Force report.

A recent Commonwealth Government report entitled *Project of National Significance: Students with Disabilities in Regular Classrooms* (1993) reinforces the importance for school systems and educational researchers of examining the role of the teacher in the inclusion of children with disabilities. The study outlined in this present proposal is therefore both relevant and timely. The findings will make a significant contribution to the understanding of an aspect of education that has become a priority in the current decade.

Research into aspects of inclusive education in Western Australia

The limited research conducted in Western Australia into aspects of inclusive education has tended to focus on children with mild to moderate intellectual disability (see, for example, Bain and Dolbel, 1991; Roberts and Naylor, 1994; Roberts and Zubrick, 1992). The inclusion of students with severe or profound disability has not attracted the attention of the local research community. This trend is consistent with the research focus in other education systems and in other nations. Within the context of the Western Australian education system this study will break new ground because it will focus exclusively on situations where the most disabled students are being included in regular classrooms.

The descriptors used by the Western Australian Education Department to categorize a child as severely or profoundly intellectually disabled are significantly different to the descriptors used to categorize a child as mildly or moderately intellectually disabled. Findings from the relatively substantial amount of research conducted into aspects of inclusive education for children with mild to moderate disabilities may not be relevant for an understanding of inclusion for students with more severe disability who present with a range of different functional characteristics. The findings from this study will go some way towards addressing this imbalance in the research focus.

The use of grounded theory

A preliminary examination of the research literature has failed to identify research studies that have used grounded theory methods to examine the way teachers manage the situation of having a child with a disability included in their class. This study is therefore uniquely placed to generate theory, grounded in data collected from rural schools in Western Australia, about this particular phenomenon.

It is anticipated that the theory that emerges from this study will be comprehensible and make sense to those teachers who will be studied. Also, the nature of grounded theory is such that the emergent theory 'will be abstract enough and include sufficient variation to make it applicable to a variety of contexts related to that phenomenon' (Strauss and Corbin, 1990: 23). In other words, the theory developed from this research will be of use to other teachers involved with inclusion, as well as other groups such as school administrators, educational policy makers, and members of the wider educational research community.

Grounded theory has been used extensively as a research methodology in sociology, and in nursing and related fields. It has been used less widely in education. This study will provide an opportunity for observations to be made about the applicability of this mode of research in education, and more specifically in the field of inclusive education.

B. The research plan

(i) The research questions

The central question of this research is as follows:

How do primary school teachers manage the situation of having a child with a severe or profound intellectual disability included in their classroom for a period of one year?

The study, and especially the data gathering process, will be guided by the following eight questions:

1. What are teachers' expectations of what is going to be involved when they realize they will have a child with a severe or profound intellectual disability in their class for the year, and what philosophical standpoint do they have about inclusion?
2. What are teachers' perceptions of the expectations of the school principal, other teachers and parents of them regarding their management of the inclusion situation? How do these perceptions change over the course of the year?

3. How does the teacher organize the classroom and education programme to accommo- date the child with the severe or profound intellectual disability, and how does this change over the course of the year?
4. What are the characteristics of the relationship between the teacher and the rest of the children in the class, and how does this relationship develop over the course of the year?
5. What are the characteristics of the relationship between the teacher and the rest of the school staff, and how does this relationship develop over the course of the year?
6. How does the teacher manage the interaction between the child with the severe or pro- found intellectual disability and other students in the class?
7. What are the characteristics of the relationship between the teacher and the parents of the child with a severe or profound intellectual disability, and how does this relationship develop during the year?
8. What relationships develop between the teacher and the parents of non-disabled children in the class? What are the characteristics of these relationships and how do they change over the course of the year?

(ii) The research method
Research design

This study will use grounded theory methodology. Grounded theory is a research method that offers a comprehensive and systematic framework for inductively building theory. A grounded theory is one that is discovered, developed, and provisionally verified through systematic data collection and analysis of data pertaining to a particular phenomenon (Strauss and Corbin, 1990). The careful and precise application of this method will ensure that the theory to emerge from this study will meet the criteria of good science: gener- alizability, reproducibility, precision, rigour, and verification (Corbin and Strauss, 1990).

A number of the basic features of grounded theory make it an appropriate method for this research. These include:

1. Grounded theory methodology specifically includes analysis of process. Within grounded theory methodology the term process is used to describe 'the linking of sequences of action/interaction as they pertain to the management of, control over, or response to, a phenomenon' (Strauss and Corbin, 1990: 143). Process is the analyst's way of accounting for or explaining change. An important aspect of this research will be to monitor the way teachers manage inclusion over the entire school year. The research questions have been constructed to guide data collection and analysis in ways that will highlight and account for any changes in teacher management as well as the ways teachers manage changing conditions that may occur during the year. In this way process will be analysed both as pro- gressive movement characterized by phases or stages, and as 'nonprogressive movement, that is, as purposeful alterations or changes in action/interaction in response to changes in conditions' (Strauss and Corbin, 1990: 52). The first conceptualization of process will involve an analysis of the conditions and corresponding actions that move the teacher

from one phase or stage of management to another. The conceptualization of process as non-progressive will involve analysis of the adjustments taken by teachers in response to changing conditions throughout the year.

2. Grounded theory methodology directly links macroscopic issues to the phenomenon under investigation. This mode of research requires that broader, contextual issues, that are shown to influence the phenomenon under study, be given appropriate recognition in the development of theory. Rather than focusing the investigation by disregarding these broader conditions, every effort will be made to acknowledge and account for them.

3. Grounded theory makes its greatest contribution in areas in which little research has been done. As stated previously, little research has been conducted specifically into aspects of the management of the inclusion of children with severe or profound intellectual disabilities in regular classrooms. Most of the research in this field has tended to focus on children with mild to moderate disabilities (for example, Center and Curry, 1993; Chambers and Kay, 1992; Deno, Maruyama, Espin and Cohen, 1990; Roberts and Zubrick, 1992), and on integration, mainstreaming, or some other form of placement that differs from inclusion (for example, Biklen, 1985; Center et al., 1988; Taylor, 1988). The paucity of research about inclusion means that many of the variables relevant to the concepts of this phenomenon are yet to be identified. Grounded theory is an appropriate methodology for this study as it will generate theory that can be used as a precursor for further investigation of this phenomenon and related issues. Other qualitative research techniques, quantitative methods, or a combination of both, can then be used in subsequent studies to test, verify or extend the qualitative hypotheses that emerge from this initial research.

The study population

The population for this study will be all primary school teachers in Western Australian country schools who, in the 1995 school year, have a child with a severe or profound intellectual disability included in their class. Information provided by the Social Justice Branch of the Education Department of Western Australia indicates that in 1994 there are 25 Government school teachers in this situation. It is anticipated that in 1995 this number will increase to approximately 28. Within the non-Government school systems (Catholic Education Commission and the Association of Independent Schools) there are approximately 10 teachers in this situation in the current year. This number is not expected to increase in 1995. It is therefore estimated that the total population for this study will be 38 teachers.

The study sample

It is estimated that approximately 25 of the 38 teachers in the study population will be in school districts in the southern half of Western Australia. For logistical reasons the gathering of data for this study will be restricted to these southern districts (Esperance, Albany, Manjimup, Bunbury North, Bunbury South, Narrogin, Peel, Northam and

Merredin). Of the 25 teachers that remain as candidates for this study, it is likely that a small proportion are unlikely to accept the invitation to become involved. This leaves a field of approximately 20 teachers.

Six teachers will be selected, at random, to provide the first body of data. This will be the initial sample group. Subsequent data collection will be guided by the theoretical sampling principle of grounded theory. Where necessary, data will be gathered from all 20 teachers if theoretical saturation on any particular category has not been achieved at an earlier stage.

In this study other decisions about the sampling process will be made during the research process itself. In a grounded theory study theoretical sampling cannot be fully planned before the study commences.

Data collection

In this study data gathering methods will include semi-structured interviews, teacher diaries, observations, and document analysis. Data will be gathered from the initial sample group in a cyclical process as outlined in the timetable below.

- Semi-structured interviews (round 1), December 1994–January 1995
- Teacher diary entries (5 days), term 1, 1995
- Semi-structured interviews (round 2), end of term 1, 1995
- Observations of teachers; 2 days per teacher (round 1), early term 2, 1995
- Teacher diary entries (5 days), early term 3, 1995
- Semi-structured interviews (round 3), early term 3, 1995
- Observations of teachers; 2 days per teacher (round 2), term 3, 1995
- Teacher diary entries (5 days), term 4, 1994
- Semi-structured interviews (round 4), term 4, 1995.

This timetable is a tentative plan for data gathering. In grounded theory studies data gathering and analysis are tightly interwoven processes; data analysis guides future data collection. Therefore, changes may be made to this provisional timetable if the analysis of data collected early in the school year indicates a need to adopt a different sequence of data gathering processes.

The precise timing of interviews, diary entries and observations will also depend on events in individual schools. It may be possible to anticipate, at the start of the school year, crucial events or periods in the school calendar that are likely to influence the way the teacher responds to the phenomenon of inclusion. These may include the first parents' meeting, the annual swimming carnival, or the first class excursion. As far as possible, data gathering activities will be timed to coincide with, or immediately follow, these school events.

Semi-structured interviews will be used as the primary means of data collection. Initially, arrangements will be made to interview each of the teachers in the initial study sample on four occasions during the course of the school year. These interviews will be tape recorded. The first round of interviews will be structured to gather data about the widest possible range of issues associated with the phenomenon under study. The research questions will guide the data gathering process. The structure and content of subsequent interviews will be determined after the data analysis process has commenced. The second, third and fourth rounds of interviews will be used to (a) gather new data about known concepts and categories that will have been developed about the phenomenon, (b) gather new data about the phenomenon, and (c) involve the teachers in a process of testing and verifying data and the emerging theory.

Each of the teachers included in the initial study sample will be requested to maintain a tape recorded diary for three periods during the year. On each of these occasions, the teacher will be encouraged to make entries into a handheld micro tape recorder for a period of five days (one school week). Every effort will be made to ensure that the teacher is comfortable with the tape diary technique and that they are clear about the purposes of this data gathering procedure.

Tape diaries serve a number of purposes (Burgess, 1984: 203). Firstly, these diaries provide first-hand accounts of situations to which the researcher may not have direct access. Secondly, they provide insiders' accounts of situations. Finally, they provide further sampling of informants, of activities and of time which may complement the observations made by the researcher.

In this study, diary entries will (a) provide the researcher with information about critical incidents that relate to the phenomenon under investigation, (b) serve as a record of the teachers' perceptions of their experiences with inclusion, (c) act as a **triangulation** strategy, and (d) stimulate and direct the data gathering process in subsequent interview sessions. The value of the link between the analysis of diary data and subsequent interviews is highlighted by Burgess (1984: 203) when he states that:

> in cases where the researcher obtains an informant's diary, it may be scanned for data that needs to be elaborated, discussed, explored and illustrated, all of which are tasks that can be conducted in an interview.

Teachers will be encouraged to keep the tape recorder with them (at home, in the car, as well as at school) throughout the five days to record as much information as possible about their experiences in managing inclusion. They will be given a brief overview of critical incident technique and encouraged to report critical incidents. They will also be advised to record their thoughts, feelings, beliefs and attitudes about these critical incidents and about the management of inclusion generally. It is anticipated that the data from each of the interviews will highlight categories that will provide a degree of focus for teachers as they use their tape diaries.

The decision to limit the periods of diary keeping to five days is based on the experiences of other researchers who have used diary techniques (see Sommer and Sommer, 1986).

The primary objective is to gather the maximum amount of relevant data without the process becoming tedious for the teacher.

The third major data gathering technique will be observation. Direct observation of how individual teachers manage the inclusion of a child with a severe or profound intellectual disability will provide the data required to verify and corroborate the information gained through interviews and diary entries. It will also allow the researcher to find cases in which there is a mismatch between interview data and teacher behaviour; where teachers do not do or act as they say they do. This will ensure that the theory generated from this research is based on more than the perceptions of teachers. School-based observations will also allow the researcher to pursue and test out relationships between theoretically relevant categories.

Initially it is planned to conduct two rounds of observations of each teacher. Once again, this may change during the course of the year depending upon the categories that emerge. Similarly, decisions about matters such as participant versus non-participant observation, timing of observations, length of observations, questioning during observation, and data recording methods will be made on a site-by-site basis.

Data will be obtained from document analysis and interviews with other members of the school communities. Arrangements will be made to interview other members of the school staff at times throughout the year. It is not possible, prior to the commencement of the data gathering process, to predict the timing of these interviews or the actual staff members to be interviewed. Education Department and school documents will also be used as sources of data. It is anticipated that such documents will provide a 'rich source of information, contextually relevant and grounded in the contexts they represent' (Lincoln and Guba, 1985: 277).

A piloting exercise will be conducted during the fourth term of the 1994 school year. A teacher with a severe or profoundly intellectually disabled child included in their class in 1994 will be invited to (a) trial the teacher diary for one week, (b) respond to, and comment on, the draft interview schedule for the first round of semi-structured interviews, and (c) comment on their experiences with inclusion during the previous three terms. This process will fine tune the data gathering methods and heighten my theoretical sensitivity towards the phenomenon of integration. Theoretical sensitivity refers to the 'attribute of having insight, the ability to give meaning to data, the capacity to understand, and capability to separate the pertinent from that which isn't' (Strauss and Corbin, 1990: 42).

Analysis of the data

Analysing data by the grounded theory method is an intricate process of reducing raw data into concepts that are designated to stand for categories. The categories are then developed and integrated into a theory (Corbin, 1986). This process is achieved by coding data, writing memos, and diagramming.

In this study, data will be coded and analysed using the three coding methods of the grounded theory model: open coding, axial coding and selective coding. Open coding is the process of breaking down, examining, comparing, conceptualizing, and categorizing data. The aim of open coding is the development of categories. Axial coding involves re-building the data (fractured through open coding) in new ways by establishing relationships between categories, and between categories and their sub-categories. Selective coding involves selecting a core category, systematically relating it to other categories, validating those relationships, and filling in categories that need further development or refinement. It is through this process that all the interpretive work done over the course of the research is integrated to form a grounded theory.

Coding procedures, memo writing and diagramming will be used as data analysis strategies. Facts or incidents obtained from interviews, documents, or diary entries, will be coded in a systematic way. Memos will be written as records of analysis, and diagrams will be developed as visual representations of the relationships between concepts. Code notes, memos and diagrams will become progressively more detailed and sophisticated as the analysis moves through the three types of coding.

Throughout the data analysis process, the teachers and other participants in the research will be involved directly in verifying the data and the emerging theory.

(iii) Efforts made to ensure that the project does not duplicate work already done

During the past six months I have conducted an extensive review of the literature in the areas of special education, integration, and inclusive education. I have been unable to locate any research that utilizes grounded theory methodology to develop a theory about how primary school teachers manage the inclusion of children with severe or profound intellectual disabilities in their regular classroom.

(iv) Confidentiality

The informed consent of the following people will be obtained prior to the commencement of the study:

1. the principals of the nominated schools;
2. the appropriate officers from the Catholic Education Commission and the Association of Independent Schools;
3. the teachers chosen in the initial sample group;
4. the parents of the children with disabilities.

The informed consent of other teachers and parents (chosen in the wider sample group) will be sought at the time they are approached to participate in the study.

All data will be treated in a way that protects the confidentiality and anonymity of the teachers, parents and children involved in the study. Coding will be used during the gathering and processing of interview notes, tapes and transcripts.

9.3 MIXED-METHOD PROPOSAL: SOCIAL MEDICINE

Name of candidate: *Claire Chinnery*

Degree: Master of Educational Studies, The University of Western Australia

Abstract

Research has demonstrated that the performance of emergency medical teams depends not only on the technical knowledge and skills of individual team members, but on generic competencies such as communication, leadership, and problem-solving. The goal of the present study is to identify factors that predict team performance in simulated cardiac arrest scenarios. The sample for the proposed study will comprise groups of health professionals attending training sessions at CTEC. Data will be collected from at least 60 teams, with approximately four members per team (total sample $n = 240$). During their standard debriefing sessions, all participants will complete a Team Composition and Process Questionnaire, which will include both closed- and open-ended questions on individual and team functioning during the scenario. Videotapes of the scenarios will then be analysed to determine the quality of each team's performance. Multiple regression analyses will be performed to test for relationships between scores on the Team Composition and Process Questionnaire and team performance ratings. Further, on the basis of the latter ratings, three poorly functioning teams will be selected for in-depth case study analysis. Videotapes for these three teams will then be analysed using the framework of activity theory to identify factors that contributed to the teams' poor task performance. The ultimate goal of the study is to provide information that may be used to improve training programmes in cardiac arrest resuscitation.

Introduction

Over the past few decades, significant efforts have been made to enhance the efficacy of training programmes in cardiac resuscitation.* Despite this, survival rates from cardiac arrest have remained relatively stable (Abella, Alvarado et al., 2005; Sanders and Ewy, 2005), even with the introduction of internationally recognized resuscitation guidelines (Sanders and Ewy, 2005). One possible reason for these poor outcomes is that health professionals fail to follow standard guidelines, resulting in delays or failures to provide the appropriate treatment (Abella, Alvarado et al., 2005; Abella, Sandbo et al., 2005; Aufderheide et al., 2004; Milander et al., 1995).

Traditionally, training for cardiac resuscitation has focused on disseminating technical knowledge and task-specific practical skills (e.g. knowledge of abnormal cardiac rhythms, appropriate use of a defibrillator). Recent perspectives on higher education have, however, highlighted the need for training programmes to foster generic competencies, as well as discipline-specific knowledge and skills. *Generic competencies* include non-technical skills that are important across all areas of a particular discipline (e.g. OECD, 2002). Given that health care delivery typically involves working as a member of a multidisciplinary team, generic competencies within this area would include skills such as communication, problem-solving, and leadership. In relation to cardiac arrest and similar medical emergencies, generic competencies may be critical for effective team performance for at least two major reasons.

First, rapid delivery of care is essential for successful resuscitation of the patient. It is generally accepted that to maximize patient survival, diagnosis and treatment should commence within three minutes of the arrest onset (Australian Resuscitation Council, 1998). Research has also indicated that as complexity in health care increases, so too do the number of errors made by health professionals (Australian Council for Safety and Quality in Health Care, 2001). In cardiac resuscitation, the need for rapid delivery, the complex and demanding nature of the treatment, and the severe implications of errors made in the delivery of the treatment, place considerable emphasis on the smooth functioning of the team managing the arrest.

Second, cardiac arrests are relatively rare. In one hospital in the UK, only 0.4% of patients were reported to have experienced a cardiac arrest (Hodgetts et al., 2002). This means that many individual health care professionals may have limited direct experience in managing cardiac arrests. Teams confronted with cardiac arrests will, therefore, often rely heavily on the distributed knowledge of all team members. By implication, the effective management of cardiac arrests will rely on factors such as the ability of team members to communicate their knowledge to others and coordinate their actions within an emergency timeframe.

Previous research on teamwork in medicine

Few studies have been conducted on the generic competencies needed by members of medical work teams in emergency situations. Of those that have, there has been an almost exclusive emphasis on the characteristics of team leaders and performance. For example, Cooper and Wakelam (1999) found that good leadership correlated positively with medical team performance in cardiac arrest situations. Several components of good leadership were identified. Overall, the ability to initiate a structure within the team was of primary importance, as it enabled the team members to work more effectively together and to perform the tasks required more efficiently. Attributes such as the ability to direct and command, to be flexible, to engender trust, and to give guidance and assistance where necessary, were found to be critical in establishing a team structure. Further key competencies of leaders included adherence to standard guidelines where appropriate, and the ability to display a positive attitude, motivate and encourage the team, decide how and when things should be done, and assign tasks to specific team members.

Other studies have supported the key facets of leadership suggested by Cooper and Wakelam (1999). In a questionnaire survey of 130 Resuscitation Training Officers in the UK, Pittman, Turner and Gabbott (2001) found that the ability to establish a team structure is important for the success of resuscitation teams. Using videotape evidence of cardiopulmonary resuscitation techniques, Mann and Heyworth (1996) also found that resuscitation tasks were performed more effectively when the team leader used standard guidelines. In a study of leadership in trauma teams, Ritchie and Cameron (1999) also ascribed many deficiencies in the performance of teams to a lack of assertive direction, poor enunciation of the overall plan, poor identification of the leader, and communication problems. In the latter study, failures by leaders to verbalize thought processes and to give clear verbal instructions were identified as particularly detrimental.

Recent research beyond medical emergencies, however, has suggested that focusing on leadership as a source of team success or failure may be too restrictive. This research has suggested that team performance may be influenced by a host of other factors such as cohesiveness, clear role divisions, and group composition factors such as gender, status and experience (e.g. Allen, Arocha and Patel, 1998; Christensen et al., 2000; Hawryluck, Espin, Garwood, Evans and Lingard, 2002; O'Donnell, Adams, DuRussel and Derry, 1997; Pagliari and Grimshaw, 2002; Strom, Strom and Moore, 1999; Vinokur, Burnstein, Sechrest and Wortman, 1985). As indicated above, some emergency medical situations such as cardiac arrest are relatively rare. As a result, even a team leader may have relatively limited experience in dealing with these situations, and thus will rely on the knowledge of other team members. Given this, effective team performance is likely to depend on a complex interplay between communication and coordination factors that do not stem solely from the actions of the team leader.

Furthermore, research within the field of medical emergencies has typically used an individualistic approach to examining team performance, rather than seeing the team as a unit of analysis. In such approaches, the assumption must be that improving the skills of individuals within the team will produce better performance by the team as a whole. While this approach has produced some insights into ways in which team performance can be improved, it has neglected overall group composition and interaction processes that may contribute to performance. The results of such research are likely to produce an overly simplistic picture of the factors that impact team outcomes. For example, much previous research suggests that team performance will hinge on characteristics of the leader. However, in emergency situations, actual (as opposed to nominal) leadership roles are often necessarily fluid. As a result, team performance cannot clearly be ascribed to only one individual within the team, as many will adopt a leadership role at different times in dealing with the emergency.

Activity theory and the study of medical emergencies

The shift to more process- and context-oriented accounts of team functioning invites the application of new tools for analysing the interactions that occur between team members. The conceptual framework provided by activity theory has clear implications for research in emergency team response contexts. From this perspective, teams are viewed *as activity systems* rather than collections of individual agents. In turn, the processes associated with responses to emergencies are viewed in terms of the activity of the team as a whole.

Activity theory has a long history within Soviet psychology, drawing on Vygotskian notions of tool mediation and sociocultural-historical theories of learning. Central to the sociocultural-historical approach is that it focuses on the analysis of the sociocultural

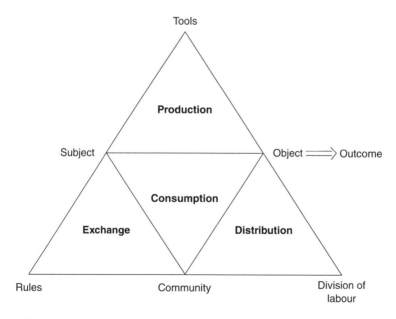

Figure 9.1 Engeström's activity system model

context rather than on the individual in isolation. Vygotsky's followers identified the *activity* as the fundamental unit of analysis. An activity refers to a goal-oriented hierarchical system of actions and operations, mediated by cultural artefacts or tools. A fundamental assumption of this approach is that activities cannot be analysed meaningfully in isolation from their social contexts. As indicated by Leontiev (1981), activity 'is not a reaction or aggregate of reactions, but a system with its own structure, its own internal transformations, and its own development' (p. 23).

These notions are further explicated and developed in the work of Engeström and his colleagues (e.g. Engeström, 1987; Engeström and Escalante, 1996). Engeström's conceptualization of activity theory emphasizes the mediating role of the community in an individual activity system. Engeström's model divides activity systems into several components (see Figure 9.1). In this model, the *subject* refers to the individual or group of individuals whose agency is chosen as the point of view in the analysis. The *object* refers to the ends towards which activity is directed (i.e. the activity that the members of the system transform into an outcome to satisfy certain needs). The *tools* mediate relationships between the subject and the object. The *community* comprises a group of interdependent people whose agency is directed at the object of the activity, and this group mediates the relationships between subject and object. The *rules* refer to the set of norms and conventions that regulate the relationships between subject and community. *Division of labour* mediates the relation between community and object, reflecting power and status within the community as well as the division of tasks between its members.

Changes within activity systems occur as a product of various inner *contradictions* that emerge within and amongst their constituent components (Engeström, 1996). *Primary* contradictions within the components of the system are responsible for the development of *need states* within the system. These need states can be resolved through the system evolving into an improved system that maintains the structure of the original by incorporating a new tool, rule, or division of labour that enables the need state to be met. Such a change is referred to as a *solution innovation*. More complex need states may have to be resolved through radical change that results in structural changes in the system. When a strong novel factor is introduced into a component of the system, it acquires a new quality, and *secondary* contradictions may appear between that component and existing components of the system. These contradictions may lead to the evolution of *tertiary* contradictions between the central form of the activity and a more advanced version of it. The activity system gradually transforms into this more advanced form to resolve the tensions that are created by such internal contradictions. These tensions may, therefore, prompt the creation of new approaches to achieving the object of the system through the development of new tools or structures that enable the system to function more cohesively.

Although the use of activity theory to analyse team processes is relatively new, this framework has been applied to examine the work of medical teams in a handful of recent studies. Engeström (2000) illustrated the potential use of activity theory to analyse interactions between nurses, physicians, and other members of medical teams in a Danish urgent care unit. A similar example is provided by Boreham, Shea and Mackway-Jones (2000), who focused on analysing the interdependencies that arise within teams in hospital emergency departments. Bardram (2000) also used activity theory to analyse the role of temporal coordination problems in hospital emergency work teams. More recently, Korpela et al. (2004) conducted an activity analysis of a medical team who were managing the treatment of a sick baby in an intensive care unit. A common theme that has emerged from all of these studies is that developing a collective understanding through the creation of shared knowledge is central to group effectiveness. Boreham et al. demonstrated further that failures to share knowledge in hospital emergency teams can have serious consequences. By implication, in order to achieve maximum effectiveness in a group situation, it is necessary to establish exactly what shared knowledge the group possesses, and assess whether this knowledge is being communicated in the most effective manner possible.

Summary and study rationale

At present, training of medical practitioners for emergency situations focuses primarily on improving technical knowledge and skills. Recent perspectives have, however, highlighted the need to include a secondary focus on generic competencies, as well as task-related knowledge and skills. This may be particularly true in emergency medical situations, where skills such as communication and problem-solving can impact performance dramatically. Further, although there has been some research on teamwork within emergency situations, it is necessary to examine the team as a whole, rather than focusing on characteristics of individuals (e.g. leaders) within the team.

In the present study, data collected during simulated cardiac arrests will be analysed to identify factors that predict team performance in emergency medical situations. A mixed-method approach will be used to address two primary research questions:

1. What are the key group composition factors (e.g. collective background experience, differentials in leadership characteristics) that predict the performance of teams in simulated cardiac resuscitation exercises? A quantitative survey approach will be used to address this goal.

2. What are the mediating links between such compositional factors and team performance? A case study approach will be used to address this goal, involving in-depth observations and analyses of the team interaction processes that occur in the simulated cardiac resuscitation exercises.

Method

Sample

The sample for the proposed study will be gathered from groups of health professionals attending training sessions at CTEC. Groups attending the centre normally include one or two doctors and three or four nurses. The groups participate in a number of emergency medical scenarios as part of their training. One of these scenarios is usually a cardiac arrest. Approximately three to four health professionals from the group would normally participate in the cardiac arrest scenario. It is expected that data collection will occur over approximately 9 months, which should allow access to at least 60 cardiac arrest scenarios (i.e. 60 teams, with approximately four members per team, total sample $n = 240$).

Setting

While simulated arrests are an accepted method of training, they have not been used extensively in research to date. In addition to the practical advantages of this approach, studying real cardiac arrests can be problematic because of the large number of factors that may impact outcomes in field situations. Many such factors will not be within the control of the team. For this reason, simulations provide a more suitable context for conducting controlled evaluations of specific team functioning and performance factors.

In the present study, all data will be collected in the high fidelity medical simulation facility at The University of Western Australia's Clinical Training and Education Centre (CTEC). The facility uses a sophisticated, computer-controlled manikin that is capable of responding to participant actions. The simulations will be conducted in a mock hospital setting with real hospital equipment. The simulated arrests will mimic real cardiac arrests as closely as possible, and participants will be asked to perform as they would in their normal professional roles.

Instruments

Team Composition and Process Questionnaire

Immediately following the simulated cardiac arrest, participants will be asked to complete the Team Composition and Process Questionnaire (see Appendix A [not reproduced]). Given that there was no established instrument available that could address the study goals, the researcher developed this questionnaire by drawing information from previous studies of group dynamics and performance outcomes. The questionnaire has two major components. The first includes a number of closed-ended subsections, designed to collect information on group demographics and perceptions of team processes.

The second uses an open-ended format designed to collect qualitative information to explain relationships between group characteristics and performance at critical points during the scenario.

Previous research in team functioning has identified a number of performance predictors that were deemed to be potentially relevant in this study. At the most general level, these are typically divided into group composition and group process factors. Composition factors that have been found to predict team performance in some situations include gender mix, age differentials, and cultural diversity (e.g. Dailey, 2003). Numerous team process factors have also been identified as potential predictors of team performance. In this study, a small number of key components were selected for inclusion on the basis of previous research in group dynamics (e.g. Doel and Sawdon, 2003; Dunn, Lewandowsky and Kirsner, 2002; Riordan and Wetherley, 1999):

- team cohesiveness (e.g. task cohesion, interpersonal cohesion, conflict);
- team processes (e.g. communication, problem-solving, and metacognition/reflection);
- team structure (e.g. salience of the cooperative task structure, collective knowledge available, role divisions within the team, and coordination of team efforts);
- leadership efficacy (e.g. decision-making, role distribution, style, communication and exchange); and
- personal characteristics of team members (e.g. sense of membership in the team, awareness of roles, personal knowledge, assertiveness, and attitudes towards teamwork).

Appendix A [not reproduced] presents the full list of items to be used in all sections of the questionnaire. The demographic checklist will be used to derive the team composition variables of interest in the study. For the closed-ended section on team processes, items are listed under conceptual category headings. In the instrument used, the items from the different subsections in this component will be interspersed. The process questions in the open-ended component of the scale are organized according to critical incidents in the resuscitation scenarios. Thus, in this section, participants will be asked to report on their actions and thought processes at key junctures during the resuscitation effort (i.e. points at which actions taken or not taken can result in the survival or death of the patient). Information from the open-ended response section will be used to map participants' perspectives on their own and on their team's performance to actual performance ratings assigned by the researcher. These ratings will be assigned during observations of video data collected for each scenario.

Video observation protocol

As part of the standard training programme at CTEC, participants are videoed during the medical emergency scenarios. The videotapes are used to facilitate discussion during a debrief after each scenario. The videotapes are normally erased at the end of each training session. For the purposes of the proposed research study, however, the videotapes will be retained for further analysis. Explicit consent for using the tapes in this manner will be sought from all participants. Based on these videos, two measures will be applied:

(i) Cardiac arrest management Task Performance Index   Each group will be rated using a previously developed index of task performance in cardiac arrest (see Appendix B [not reproduced]). The index gives a numerical score to each team based on correct and timely use of the accepted protocol for management of cardiac arrest. The interrater reliability of the index will be estimated during the proposed using a sample of 5% of all videos. A criterion level of 85% agreement will be adopted before the observations proceed.

(ii) Team Process Transcriptions   Three low scoring groups with different kinds of profiles on the quantitative Team Composition and Process Questionnaire will be selected for the in-depth case study observations. Videos for these three groups will then be transcribed both for the actions taken and for interactions between team members in a running event record format (Heath and Vom Lehn, 2000).

Procedure

All groups attending training sessions at CTEC will be invited to participate in the study. Participants will be given verbal and written information relating to the study. Written consent will be obtained from those who wish to participate. Consent will state explicitly that videos will be retained for the purpose of analysis by the researcher only, and that their anonymity will be preserved in the presentation of the study results. Trainers involved in running the training sessions will be briefed on the requirements of the study and will distribute the questionnaires following cardiac arrest scenarios. Each participant in the cardiac arrest scenario will be identified by a number pinned to his or her clothing and written on the questionnaire. This will enable correlation of data from questionnaires and video transcriptions. The completed questionnaires and videotape from each scenario will be sealed in an envelope and stored in a locked cupboard to be collected by the researcher for analysis.

Data analysis

Two different types of analyses will be used to address the two research questions.

Research question 1 will be addressed using quantitative analysis methods. To identify which group composition and process variables contributed significantly to predicting team performance, a multiple regression analysis will be performed. In this analysis, the criterion (dependent) variable will be group scores on the Task Performance Index. The unit of analysis will be team performance, rather than individual scores. The predictor (independent) variables will be the indices of team composition and process derived from members of each team. These will be combined (e.g. averaged) to form group-level indices for inclusion in the analysis. Using the summed scores for each of the dimensions in the Team Composition and Process Questionnaire, there will be four composition predictors (e.g. collective background experience of each team) and six process predictors (e.g. overall cohesiveness score). Given overall $n = 60$ (i.e. $n > 5$ cases per predictor), the statistical power of associated inferential tests will be within acceptable ranges.

Research question 2 will be addressed through qualitative analysis of the cases selected for this phase. To identify the mediating links between the group composition/process variables and team performance, data collected in the Team Process Transcriptions and the open-ended component of the Team Composition and Process Questionnaire will be integrated to identify potential explanatory themes that emerge with respect to group dysfunction.

As noted by Engeström (2000), activity theory does not offer ready-made techniques and procedures for research. Instead, it provides conceptual tools that must be applied according to the specifics and nature of the objective of the activity under scrutiny. Engeström does, however, present the following two principles for conducting an activity-based analysis:

1. Focus on a collective activity system as the unit of analysis. Once the collective activity system has been established, identify components and attributes of that system.
2. Identify all sources of contradictions 'within' and 'between' the various components of the collective activity system. According to Engeström, contradictions form the basis of new understandings about the activity system being investigated.

In this study, the event records will first be analysed for evidence of contradictions arising from tool use, divisions of labour, and application of rules based on the researcher's observations. The open-ended responses made by each participant will then be analysed to explore individuals' perspectives on the extent to which their performance was impacted by the tools available and the manner in which these were used, the adequacy of the rules they attempted to follow in the situation, and the divisions of labour within the team. Thus the analysis of the open-ended responses will lend itself to two levels of conclusions: one relating to the contradictions in the perspectives of individuals and observed events, the second relating to the inner contradictions between the components of the activity system.

In the observations of the videos, key dimensions will include conflict processes, role divisions and specializations, patterns of dominance and status, and task characteristic/group composition factors. A coding scheme will be developed to identify themes that emerge in the team exchanges and dialogues. This scheme will focus on the types of exchanges that occur in response to specific events in the teamwork context. For example, in coding the associated verbal exchanges, members' statements will be coded as initiations, elaborations, integrations, modifications, maintenance, clarification seeking, or disengagement bids. This method of structural analysis is well validated within the sociocultural-historical tradition.

Ethical considerations

Ethics approval will be sought from The University of Western Australia human ethics committee. As previously stated, all participants will be informed verbally and in writing about the study and participation will be on a voluntary basis. Written consent to participate will be obtained from those who volunteer and participants may withdraw from the study at any time. Raw data including videos, questionnaires, and transcripts will be stored securely for the appropriate period of time according to the requirements of the ethics committee.

Note

*A cardiac arrest occurs when a patient's heart ceases to beat in the organized manner required to circulate blood around the body. There are four disturbances of the normal heart rhythm that can cause cardiac arrest. Two of these, ventricular tachycardia and ventricular fibrillation, can be successfully reversed in the majority of patients if rapid detection and appropriate resuscitation occur. The other disturbances, asystole and pulseless electrical activity, are less amenable to treatment but can still be reversed in some cases. Hospital-based treatment of cardiac arrest includes cardiac compressions, defibrillation, advanced airway management and the administration of drugs. Together, these interventions are often called Advanced Life Support.

9.4 QUANTITATIVE PROPOSAL: MANAGEMENT/BUSINESS

Name of candidate: *Tim Mazzarol*

Degree: Doctor of Philosophy, Curtin University of Technology

1 Abstract

It is proposed to undertake a research study to examine the factors critical to the establishment and maintenance of sustainable competitive advantage for education service enterprises in international markets. A model of sustainable competitive advantage for service enterprises in international markets has been developed following an examination of current literature. This model will be tested via a survey encompassing all Australian institutions, and a further 100 overseas institutions drawn equally from the United States, United Kingdom, Canada and New Zealand. This will be supplemented by a detailed examination of approximately six Australian institutions using a case study approach.

The survey method will involve a mailout questionnaire designed to measure the responses of key decision makers in the sample institutions. This questionnaire will capture information reflecting the perceptions and practice of those guiding the export strategy of education institutions. It will serve as a means of evaluating the validity of the research model. Data analysis will be made using causal path analysis aided by computer packages such as LISREL and SPSS. The case studies will be undertaken via personal interviews with key decision makers within the selected institutions.

A pilot survey is currently being field tested, with a full survey to follow in late 1994, early 1995. The case studies will be undertaken in early 1995 via interviews. Data analysis will take place during 1995, with an anticipated completion of the thesis by late 1996.

Objectives

The overall objectives of this research may be summarized as follows:

1. Examine the effects of external environmental variables (industry and foreign market structure) on marketing strategies within education service exporters.
2. Evaluate the importance of specific marketing strategy outcomes to the generation of competitive advantage for education service providers within international markets.
3. Evaluate the ability of education service providers to generate barriers to the imitation of strategies offering competitive advantage.
4. Examine the long term market and financial performance of education service providers in international markets as an outcome of the interaction between marketing strategies (offering sources of competitive advantage), and the ability of the enterprise to sustain such advantage in the face of imitation.

2 Background

Australian schools and universities have educated foreign students for over 100 years, but until the mid 1980s, most of these students came to Australia through overseas aid programmes such as the Colombo Plan (DCT, 1993: 38). In 1985 the Federal Government opened the nation's education system to full-fee-paying foreign students with a view to tapping the estimated world student market of 1 million (Kemp, 1990). From an initial 4,503 in 1986, the size of Australia's intake of overseas students has grown rapidly to

47,882 in 1991 (AGB, 1992). These students generate hundreds of millions of dollars in export income via fees and services, and help support around 970 institutions (Industry Commission, 1991: 39).

Despite the relative success of Australia's education exports, concern has been expressed over the lack of comprehensive research into the marketing of such services (Marshall and Smart, 1991). A recent survey of international students and their advisers found their knowledge of Australia as an education destination mixed (AGB, 1992). There was a lack of knowledge about the country and its institutions even though quality was generally viewed as 'probably acceptable'. In some markets, notably Korea, Australia's image was quite poor (AGB, 1992). The problem was summarized as follows:

> Australia has no clear differentiation on product offerings, i.e. it is not perceived as the 'best' destination for any particular study disciplines. This contrasts with perceptions about the USA and the UK which have established particular discipline strengths in the minds of respondents. (AGB, 1992: 2)

Many of Australia's education exporters entered the market offering a relatively undifferentiated service, attractive primarily due to its low cost and generous work provisions within the visa regulations (Smart and Ang, 1992a; Industry Commission, 1991). The majority of Australia's overseas students have been drawn from a narrow range of markets. Malaysia and Singapore, for example, represent over two-thirds of the total students enrolled in Western Australia (DCT, 1993: 44). This poses long term sustainability problems should these markets experience a contraction due to political, social or economic change. Research also suggests that the world wide flow of students has declined rapidly since the 1980s (Kemp, 1990), raising additional questions about future industry growth.

3 Significance of This Research

This research is significant because it addresses a need – as outlined above – for comprehensive research into the international marketing of education. Past literature relating to the export of education has examined the economic or socio-political aspects of the industry rather than marketing (Smart and Ang, 1992b). Furthermore, despite a rapid growth in services marketing literature during the past decade (Fisk, Brown and Bitner, 1993), research into the international marketing of services remains limited (Nicoulaud, 1989; Dahringer, 1991; Erramilli and Rao, 1990; Erramilli, 1990; 1991).

Both services and international marketing are relatively new academic fields and were not given serious consideration prior to the 1970s (Terpstra, 1987; Berry and Parasuraman, 1993). With the growth in both international trade and the services sectors of most industrialized nations during the 1970s and 1980s (Blois, 1974; Plunkert, 1990; Roach, 1991; Terpstra, 1987), interest in these two fields grew. However, there remains a dearth of literature relating to the international marketing of services. It is hoped that this research will make a significant contribution to enhancing the level of knowledge in this area.

Of equal importance is how to develop strategies that will ensure the sustainability of competitive advantage for education service exporters so as to offer long term stability for this important industry. Academic research into sustainable competitive advantage for services industries remains at a rudimentary level with little applied research having been undertaken (Bharadwaj, Varadarajan and Fahy, 1993). Once again this research should make a significant contribution to enhancing the level of understanding relating to this.

Although the primary focus of this research will be on the education export industry, it is anticipated that the findings of this study will be applicable to most other services exporters. It is therefore the intention of this research to develop models and conclusions that will be generic to international services marketing.

Because it is proposed to survey virtually all Australian institutions engaged in the export of education, this study will provide valuable insights into the current perceptions and marketing practices of the industry. It has the potential to serve as a bench mark study of current practice. To this end it should prove of interest and value to practising managers and those seeking to implement international marketing strategies for education institutions.

4 Research methodology

4.1 The research model

Figure 9.2 illustrates a model of sustainable competitive advantage for service enterprises in international markets developed from a number of established theories relating to competitive advantage, international marketing and services marketing research (Aaker, 1989, 1992; Barney, 1986, 1991; Booms and Bitner, 1981; Cowell, 1984; Dahringer, 1991; Gronroos, 1990; Klein and Roth, 1990; Nicoulaud, 1987; Porter, 1980, 1985; Porter and Fuller, 1986; Porter and Millar, 1985).

As a model of sustainable competitive advantage it assumes that business and marketing strategies within the enterprise are determined by external environmental factors to which the enterprise responds. It is consistent with the theoretical framework offered by Porter (1980, 1985). An alternative perspective is that proposed by Bharadwaj, Varadarajan & Fahy (1993), which views the achievement of sustainable competitive advantage resulting from the enterprise selecting critical sources of competitiveness from among internal resources and skills.

The elements of the model can be briefly summarized as follows:

- *Industry structure.* Describes the external forces influencing the industry within which the enterprise operates. Porter (1980) defines these as: (1) barriers to entry; (2) supplier power; (3) buyer power; (4) threat of substitutes; (5) industry competitiveness.
- *Foreign market structure.* Includes tariff and non-tariff barriers to entry (Dharinger, 1991; Onkvisit and Shaw, 1988) as well as the degree of *psychic distance* (cultural similarity/

dissimilarity) and *experience* (level of market knowledge/information) (Erramilli, 1991; Goodnow and Hansz, 1972; Klein and Roth, 1990).

- *Generic enterprise strategy.* This adopts Porter's (1985) theory that all enterprises must adopt one of three *generic* strategies in order to achieve a competitive advantage. These three strategies are: (1) *cost leadership* (competing via cost); (2) *differentiation* (competing via uniqueness); and (3) *focus* (competing via cost or differentiation within a niche market) (Porter, 1985).

- *External marketing strategy.* Describes the specific marketing strategies relating to the *marketing mix* which incorporates considerations of the following: (1) product/service development; (2) pricing; (3) distribution; (4) promotion; and development of physical evidence of the service (buildings, equipment) (McCarthy, 1960; Booms and Bitner, 1981).

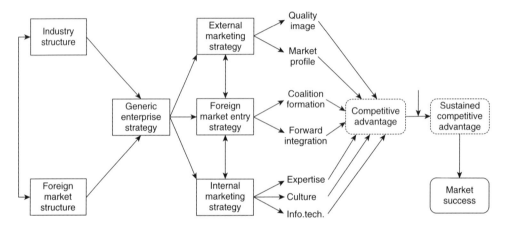

Figure 9.2 Model of sustainable competitive advantage for service enterprises in international markets

- *Foreign market entry strategy.* Describes the methods used to enter a foreign market. These are identified as: (1) direct export; (2) licensing; (3) franchising; (4) joint venture; (5) acquisition; and (6) management contracting (Cowell, 1984). Also examines the degree of control exercised by the enterprise over its marketing channel (Anderson and Coughlan, 1987).

- *Internal marketing strategy.* Describes the processes undertaken within the enterprise to foster an organizational culture that is both client service oriented (Flipo, 1985; Gronroos, 1990), and encouraging of innovation (Ansoff, 1987; Barney, 1986; Foster and Pryor, 1986; Ghemawat, 1986; Kanter, 1989). Also considers the enterprise approach to the recruitment and retention of experienced and talented staff, and their performance via various service delivery processes (Booms and Bitner, 1981; Lovelock, 1983; Thomas, 1978).

- *Outcomes.* The outcomes of enterprise marketing strategies identified within the model are considered of critical importance to the establishment of competitive advantage for services enterprises in international markets. These are: (1) quality of image; (2) market profile (consumer awareness or knowledge of enterprise) (Aaker, 1989; Hill and Neeley, 1988); (3) coalition formation (strategic alliances) (Dunning and Pearce, 1985; Ohmae, 1985; Porter and Fuller, 1986); (4)

degree of forward integration into the marketing channel (Erramilli and Rao, 1990; Erramilli, 1990; Nicoulaud, 1987; Vanermere and Chadwick, 1989); (5) level of staff expertise and organizational learning (Winter, 1987); (6) organizational culture as client oriented and innovative (Quinn, 1980; 1985); and (7) effective use of information technology (Porter and Millar, 1985).

- *Barriers to imitation*. To ensure that competitive advantage is sustained it is suggested (Bharadwaj, Varadarajan and Fahy, 1993) that the enterprise erect barriers to the imitation of its strategies. A variety of possible barriers have been identified in the literature (Coyne, 1985; Dierickx and Cool, 1989; Lippman and Rumelt, 1982; Rumelt, 1984; 1987; Reed and Defillippi, 1990).
- *Market success*. The model assumes that the concepts *competitive advantage* and *sustainable competitive advantage* cannot be measured directly. Instead the measurement of market success is achieved via the dual outcomes of (1) market share and (2) profitability (financial performance).

4.2 Hypotheses

The relationships that will be tested in the model can be identified in the following hypotheses:

H1	Industry structure is a determinant of generic enterprise strategy adopted by a service enterprise seeking competitive advantage in international markets.
H2	Foreign market structure is a determinant of generic enterprise strategy adopted by a service enterprise seeking competitive advantage in international markets.
H3	Generic enterprise strategy is a moderating variable that determines: (a) the external marketing strategy of the enterprise; (b) the foreign market entry strategy of the enterprise; (c) the internal marketing strategy of the enterprise.
H4	External marketing strategy is a moderating variable that enables the creation of sources of competitive advantage for a service enterprise within an international market.
H5	Foreign market entry strategy is a moderating variable that enables the creation of sources of competitive advantage for a service enterprise within an international market.
H6	Internal marketing strategy is a moderating variable that enables the creation of sources of competitive advantage for a service enterprise within an international market.
H7	The key intervening variables that strengthen the competitive advantage of a service enterprise within an international market are: (a) quality of image; (b) market profile; (c) coalition formation; (d) degree of forward integration into the export channel; (e) organizational expertise and quality of staff; (f) possession of a client-oriented/innovative culture; (g) effective use of information technology.
H8	Sustainability of competitive advantage is only achievable if there are intervening variables which act as barriers to imitation. The most likely barriers are: (a) the external marketing strategy of the enterprise; (b) the foreign market entry strategy of the enterprise; (c) the internal marketing strategy of the enterprise.

4.3 Sample plan

It is proposed to survey all education institutions in Australia that are accredited to the Department of Education, Employment and Training (DEET) as exporters. DEET maintains a Commonwealth Register of Institutions and Courses (CRICOS) listing all such institutions in Australia. DEET has provided a complete listing including telephone numbers and addresses. This listing includes around 1,000 institutions ranging from small training colleges to large universities. This will form the basis of the Australian sample and has already proven of value in conducting the pilot study.

In addition to the Australian institutions, an additional 100 institutions in each of four overseas countries (USA, UK, Canada and New Zealand) will be sampled. Details of institutions within these countries are available from the various diplomatic and consular agencies located in Australia. Initial contact with the British Council, Canadian High Commission, US Consulate and New Zealand High Commission has proven fruitful in identifying suitable institutions likely to form a sample.

Non-English-speaking countries have been ignored due to the added complexities and cost of developing a foreign language survey. Traditionally, the primary competition to Australian education institutions are other English-speaking nations, although Germany, France and Japan are emerging as significant competitors in Australian markets (Smart and Ang, 1992b). Nevertheless, it is felt that sufficient validity within the sample will be achieved using the English-speaking nations alone.

Selection of the case study sample (estimated to be approximately six institutions) will be on the basis of size, institution type and relative experience within the international market. The aim will be to select a cross-section of institutions which represent these elements. A suggested case study sample would be likely to include: (1) a large university; (2) a commercial business/training college; (3) a private secondary school; (4) an English language college; (5) a TAFE/technical training college; (6) a specialist training institution (e.g. pilot training).

4.4 Instrumentation and data collection

A copy of the questionnaire as used in the pilot study is attached [not reproduced]. Prior to forwarding, a contact person within each institution is to be identified. A pre-paid envelope will be included with each questionnaire sent. Respondents will be offered a summary of findings from the study as a courtesy. This approach has been adopted in the pilot study with success.

4.5 Data analysis

Due to the relatively large number of variables in the research model, analysis will be made using causal path modelling (Saris & Stonkhorst, 1984). This will enable the relationships between the variables in the model to be solved as a **multivariate** regression equation, and will permit the examination of both observed and unobserved (**latent**) variables (Loehlin, 1992).

Data analysis will be facilitated using the LISREL computer software package operating in conjunction with SPSS (Byrne, 1989). Both software packages operate under the MS Windows environment on an IBM compatible PC. The LISREL package will allow a statistical comparison of the data and the research model (Byrne, 1989).

9.5   QUALITATIVE PROPOSAL: NURSING

Name of candidate: *Kay Price*

Degree: Doctor of Philosophy, The University of South Australia

1 Title

The construction of pain within a surgical ward.

2 Purpose of the study

Pain management is an aspect of post-operative care which is, or is perceived as, being poorly managed by health care professionals (e.g. U.S. Department of Health and Human Services, 1992; Owen, McMillan and Rogowski, 1990; Winefield, Katisikitis, Hart and Rounsefell, 1990; Edwards, 1990; Kilham, Atkinson, Bogduk, Cousins, Hodder, Pilowsky, Pollard and Quinn, 1988; Liebeskind and Melzack, 1987). This being despite a view heralded within the literature that advances in the understanding of pain mechanisms, the action of analgesic drugs and the development of sophisticated systems for drug delivery, mean that it is no longer necessary for the surgical client to suffer from unrelieved pain post-surgery (e.g. U.S. Department of Health and Human Services, 1992; Owen and Cousins, 1991; Kilham et al., 1988; Mather and Phillips, 1986). Unrelieved pain has personal, social and economic costs. For example, the experience of unrelieved pain has been linked to the surgical client experiencing complications, thus increasing their length of stay in hospital which ultimately requires the allocation of additional resources (e.g. Ready, 1991; Benedetti, 1990). While the experience of unrelieved pain has been recognized as an undesirable occurrence for surgical clients, the provision of appropriate pain management for surgical clients remains a contentious issue.

This study is based on the belief that a certain way of thinking and speaking about pain dominates the management of a surgical client's potential or actual experience of pain at the exclusion of (or silencing of) other ways of thinking and speaking. The potential or actual experience of pain has become a means through which dominant knowledge sources and power relations are maintained and produced through its management. Abercrombie, Hill and Turner (1988: 71) define a 'domain of language use that is unified by common assumptions' as a discourse. The notion of discourse and the way in which it shapes the form and content of language both written and spoken has been extensively explored by Foucault (1977). His notion of discourse and his analyses of discursive frameworks provide an understanding of the interplay between power, knowledge and discourses (Cheek and Rudge, 1993). Pain and its management have become discursively constructed. Within this discursive construction exists the interplay of other discursive constructions which offer competing, potentially contradictory ways of positioning its author(s), all of which vary in authority (Gavey, 1989: 464). The 'authors' of these discursive constructions and the positioning they adopt in relation to other discourses in pain management need to be identified if effective management from a client-centred approach is to be a reality of practice.

Thus this study aims to explore and explicate:

1. the way in which pain is constructed within a surgical ward;
2. the effect(s) of this construction on nursing practice; and
3. the influences of this construction on client outcomes.

Guided by poststructuralist theory this critical study will, by using ethnographic techniques and discourse analysis, represent, interrogate, juxtapose and construct the experience of pain for surgical clients. In so doing, it is envisaged that client satisfaction with their pain management will be enhanced.

The objectives of this study are to:

1. explore the various construction(s) of pain within a surgical ward of an acute care hospital and within the literature;
2. interview nursing staff, doctors and clients in regard to the work they perform in acute pain management;
3. observe the clinical practices of nursing staff and doctors within a surgical ward as they relate to the acute pain management of a surgical client;
4. analyse the documentation that reflects the care provided to surgical clients in acute pain management;
5. articulate the influence on nursing practice in light of the above understandings; and thus
6. reflect a view that highlights the consequences of all of the above on client outcomes in acute pain management following surgery.

3 Background and preliminary studies

Research studies in acute pain management have generated the dominant view that post-surgical clients experience a high incidence of unrelieved pain (Owen, McMillan and

Rogowski, 1990; Winefield, Katisikitis, Hart and Rounsefell, 1990; Carr, 1990; Donovan, Dillon and McGuire, 1987; Cohen, 1980). Unrelieved post-operative pain is considered a significant health problem (Cousins and Mather, 1989; Benedetti, 1990; Ready, 1991; Owen and Cousins, 1991). The focus of research reports has tended to concentrate on the attributes of medical and nursing staff as correlates to poor pain management (e.g. Bonica, 1980; Kilham et al., 1988; Mather and Phillips, 1986; McKingley and Bolti, 1990; McCaffery, 1990; McCaffery and Ferrell, 1991, 1992, 1994). As well, it has been stated that treatment options for post-operative pain would be ineffective in environments which had logistic and administrative hurdles (Owen et al., 1990: 306; Cousins and Mather, 1989: 355). The view [of] 'freedom' from acute pain without demand for such freedom has been suggested as a 'right' of surgical clients (e.g. Liebeskind and Melzack, 1988; Madjar, 1988).

There is literature which reflects the view that nursing has been constructed by powerful discourses including those of medicine and gender, thus marginalizing a nursing discourse (e.g. Cheek and Rudge, 1994; Parker and Gardner, 1992; Street, 1992; Bruni, 1989). Research by Street (1992: 2) into nursing practice has been described as a study in which:

> The culture of nursing is reclaimed … as a site in which the intersection of power, politics, knowledge, and practice gives rise to the contested terrain of conflict and struggle.

Street (1992: 276) believed that nursing care was essentially nurturant and that her research would enable nurses 'to recognise the politics that constrain and oppress' the clinical practice of nurses.

What influence the view that a discourse of nursing has been marginalized has on nursing practice in routine acute pain management situations remains to be explored. It is known that acute pain management for surgical clients involves a number of health care professionals, predominantly medical and nursing personnel who share responsibility for the quality of care the surgical client receives, and the financial costs involved in the delivery of this care. As a consequence of this shared responsibility there is the potential for divergence of opinion as to how the surgical client is to be most appropriately managed, which will influence client outcomes as well as affect nursing practice. Further to this, studies into clients' participation in their own care (Strauss, Fagerhaugh, Suczek and Weiner, 1982) have revealed that the work of clients in hospitals is often unrecognized and taken for granted. While clients are judged on their ability to carry out certain 'tasks', this is conceived as participation in the work of health care professionals rather than the work of clients (Strauss et al., 1982: 979). It is unknown how nurses and doctors conceive the work of clients in acute pain management.

The predominant view within the literature on pain is that proposed scientific discoveries in pain management only await application by health care professionals (e.g. Owen et al., 1990) and that following universal acceptance pain management for clients will improve. The difficulty in accepting such a view is not a rejection of the achievements made, but the limited critique of the power that the dominant positivist, empiricist research tradition presumes and the effects this power exerts on the way of knowing promoted and the subsequent management of clients by health care professionals, particularly nurses.

Code (1991: 159) writes:

> Scientific achievement is at once wonderful and awful: it can never be evaluated merely as knowledge for its own sake, for there are always political implications.

The political implications of scientific achievements in pain management have received minimal debate within the literature reviewed on pain and its management. This is not surprising given that research in the main has evolved from the dominant positivist, empiricist research tradition. A noted exception to this is the early work of Fagerhaugh and Strauss (1977) who explored the politics of pain management from a grounded theory approach.

Fagerhaugh and Strauss (1977: 9) argued that pain management took place within an organizational and interactional context, and maintained that pain management had profoundly political aspects. They (Fagerhaugh and Strauss, 1977: 8–9) suggest that people enter highly politicized arenas when they enter hospital and that while staff make and enforce the 'basic rules', staff are neither all-powerful nor completely in control of all issues which affect clients. Consequently, they believed that medical and nursing care involved politicized action. As a result of their study, Fagerhaugh and Strauss (1977: 69) believed that a critical examination of pain management in routine situations was necessary so as to improve accountability of all concerned, and prevent the phenomenon of problem pain patients. It is significant to note that Fagerhaugh and Strauss (1977) did not address specifically the influence of power relations on pain management; rather they focused on personal pain philosophies of nurses and doctors as being a key determinant of client outcomes.

The theme 'politics of health-talk' has been researched by Fox (1993). In his study, Fox was interested in discourse and its consequences for power, control and knowledge-ability. His interest was on discerning a difference between modern and postmodern theories of health, in particular the practical politics and ethics of health, and produced the view that generating new positions and resisting existing discourses was essential. Nettleton (1992), in her studies on dentistry, researched the technique of disciplinary power – the dental examination – as a means by which bodies are observed and analysed. In her study, Nettleton explored dental practices to show the relations between dental knowledge and dental power.

The definition of pain which is commonly cited in the literature is that 'pain is what the person says hurts' (Kilham et al., 1988). This definition assumes not only the authenticity of the experience as expressed by the person, but their ability to express the experience and for this to be heard (and/or observed) by nurses and doctors. Furthermore, Fox (1993: 144) writes about the 'politics of pain' and states that pain as a sensation has no meaning, the self is the pain and the self is the effect of the meaning. These perspectives require that an understanding of how pain is constructed by nurses, doctors and clients be undertaken. For as much as Fox (1993) and Nettleton (1992) have generated new viewing positions in relation to health and dentistry, thus resisting existing discourses, a similar situation needs to be explored in acute pain management.

Thus this study seeks to build upon the research of Fagerhaugh and Strauss (1977), by applying a poststructuralist framework to acute pain management for the surgical client. The interest of this study is to explore the social construction of pain by the major care providers in an acute post-operative ward, namely nurses and doctors.

4 Subjects: selection and exclusion criteria

The setting for this study will be a general adult surgical ward of an acute care public hospital. The actual location of the study setting will be negotiated with the hospital hierarchy and in full consultation with all staff members of the ward. Given the diversity of compounding factors which could influence the outcomes of this study, the setting will not be an orthopaedic ward given the likelihood of trauma causing the reason for surgery. Permission will be sought from the hospital hierarchy to locate the study within a ward that focuses on abdominal and/or thoracic surgery. Nursing, medical and client personnel working within such a setting will be invited to participate by consenting to being interviewed and observed in their work. The interactions (written and verbal) that take place in relation to the acute pain management of surgical clients will be the focus of the study. A perceived difficulty of the study will be the ability of surgical clients during the acute phase of their surgical admission, and the availability of medical and nursing staff to participate in the interview process.

As in all ethnographic studies, it will be necessary for the researcher to ensure the appropriateness and adequacy of information needed to achieve the aims of the study. It is difficult therefore to be precise about the selection and sample of informants. Control of the selection of informants may be necessary. In the event that interviews of any one group prove to be difficult, a survey by the use of a questionnaire will be adopted. Any additional informant identified by the researcher as having particular knowledge deemed as necessary for inclusion in the study will be approached to participate. These biases will be used as a 'tool' to facilitate the research study.

The decision to focus the study in an adult acute care public hospital has been based on the professional and personal experiences of the researcher.

These experiences have led to the belief that there are varying approaches to care in the management of children and adults in acute pain management. As well, that the role of medical and nursing personnel in the private sector is different to that of the public sector. It is envisaged that further research will follow from this study to address the basis for these beliefs.

While the success of the study depends upon the willingness of individuals to participate, if at any time such participation places an individual at risk or causes undue stress, participation will not be pursued. A particular concern of this researcher is not to interfere with the recovery of surgical clients and the nursing and medical practices needed to facilitate this recovery. If observations and/or interviews of either clients, nurses or doctors are deemed inappropriate, alternative methods (e.g. survey questionnaire) to gather information will be adopted.

5 Study plan and design

Ethnographic research techniques aim to generate descriptions for the purpose of analysis. Working from an insider's (nurses, doctors and surgical clients) knowledge and experience of acute pain management will provide the means for the exploration of how pain is constructed and how the construction of pain influences nursing practice and client outcomes. The question for this study is:

How is pain constructed within a surgical ward? An ongoing review of the literature will take place throughout the study which will incorporate the following stages.

Stage 1

The first stage of this research will include:

1. Gaining human ethics committee approval for the research project.
2. Negotiating access to the setting for the study.
3. Meeting with the nursing and medical staff of the general surgical ward to discuss the research, its aims and objectives; to process consent; and to provide any additional information as requested. It will be particularly important to discuss with nursing and medical staff the role of the researcher during those times of observation on the ward. Ethical considerations are discussed in more detail in Section 7 of this proposal.
4. Seeking the consent of medical and nursing staff of the general surgical ward to be interviewed and observed (written and verbal) in their practice.
5. Establish rapport with the nursing and medical staff of the general surgical ward so as to establish guidelines for observation of their practices.

Stage 2

The second stage of the research (over a period of 4–6 months) will include:

1. Observation of nursing, medical and/or clients' work in acute pain management during: admission procedures; ward rounds (nursing and/or medical); nursing handovers; and direct client care by either nursing and/or medical staff to surgical clients. Section 7 of this proposal discusses ethical considerations in relation to the role of the researcher during observation. Observation of clients will encompass that time from admission to the surgical ward until discharge.
2. Selection and interview (formal and informal) of nursing and medical staff involved in client care and surgical clients admitted to the general surgical ward during the period of the study. Interviews will mainly be informal and will occur at a time convenient to staff and clients during observation and at prearranged times during the course of the study. Surgical clients who give consent to participate in the study, dependent upon their health status, will be interviewed on admission, post-surgery and on discharge. The number of times a surgical client will be interviewed post-surgery will be dependent upon their length of stay in hospital and will take place at a time that has been mutually agreed by the client and nursing and medical staff. Initially the interviews will be **unstructured**, and as the study progresses more structured interviews will be arranged with the consent of informants. With the permission of informants, interviews may be taped and transcribed. All information provided in the interviews and during observation will be treated in strictest confidence, and transcriptions of observations and interviews will be given to informants for review to ensure that their views have been accurately represented. The interviews will focus on the informants' views about: their feelings; events; and incidents that have occurred as related to acute pain management.
3. Review of nursing and medical documentation surrounding surgical clients' stay in hospital as it relates to acute pain management. Permission to access clients' case-notes will be obtained prior to the review of the same and pseudonyms will be used so as to ensure confidentiality.
4. Collation of data obtained from observation and interviews and the provision of such data to informants at regular interviews as is appropriate.

Stage 3

This stage of the study will occur concurrently with stage 2, and will include:

1. Analysis of documentation such as nursing care plans, client case-notes and related literature on acute pain management.
2. Analysis of observations of medical, nursing and clients' work in acute pain management.
3. Analysis through interviews of medical, nursing and clients' perceptions of acute pain management.
4. Interrelationship of all the analyses on the construction(s) of pain within the general surgical ward, and the potential implications for nursing practice and client outcomes.

6 Efficacy

Not applicable.

7 Ethical considerations

Informants' needs will take precedence over the actual process of the research. While the success of the study depends upon the willingness of individuals to participate, if at any time such participation places an individual at risk or causes undue stress, participation will not be pursued. A particular concern of this researcher is not to interfere with the recovery of surgical clients and the nursing and medical practices needed to facilitate this recovery. If observations and/or interviews of either clients, nurses or doctors are deemed inappropriate, alternative methods (e.g. survey questionnaire) to gather information will be adopted.

Gaining access to the study's setting will involve negotiations with hospital hierarchy so as to determine in which adult general surgical ward the study will be based. Following this determination, a meeting of the medical and nursing staff of the surgical ward will take place. Given the busy schedules of these personnel, it may be desirable to hold separate meetings with medical and nursing staff to discuss the study. At these meetings, it will be stressed that:

1. Participation in this study will be entirely voluntary for all informants.
2. At all times, every potential informant will have communicated to her/him the objectives of the research and any change that may occur in these objectives during the course of the study. An information sheet (Appendices 1 and 2 [not reproduced]), will be provided to all potential informants.
3. Continuous and negotiated permission to observe and/or interview medical staff, nursing staff and clients will take place. Consent, either written or verbal, will be obtained prior to any aspect of the study. Informants who wish to give written consent to observation of their practice/work in acute pain management and/or interviews at the beginning of the study will be informed that they can withdraw at any time during the study (Appendix 3 [not reproduced]).

Given the ongoing nature of the study, a proposal for process consent will be suggested. 'A process consent offers the opportunity to actualize a negotiated view and to change arrangements if necessary. A process consent encourages mutual participation' (Munhall, 1991: 267). The process consent will be discussed with all potential nursing and medical staff informants at the initial meeting. Arrangements to be negotiated will include:

1. lines of communication between the researcher, informants and hospital hierarchy;
2. location of interviews;
3. length of time for interviews;

4. how information will be treated (confidentiality and anonymity);
5. taping of interviews;
6. reviewing of transcripts;
7. what will be done with unanticipated findings;
8. how secrets and confidential information will be treated;
9. possibility of group interviews;
10. when and how progress of the study will occur and be reported;
11. publishing of findings;
12. presentation of the study's progress by the researcher to doctoral review panel.

It is important to highlight that the researcher will not be delivering care to clients. The Faculty of Nursing has a Clinical Facilitation agreement with hospitals and the conditions of this agreement will be adhered to by the researcher. As a registered nurse, the researcher will only intervene in emergency situations, that is, where the life and safety of the client is at risk. Consequently, it will be essential for the researcher to establish clear guidelines, as per the Clinical Facilitation agreement, with nursing and medical staff in relation to situations where the researcher observes what she perceives to be inappropriate (or unsafe) delivery of care to clients. Mechanisms for reporting action to be taken in such situations will be clarified at the first meeting and renegotiated with nursing and medical staff as is necessary.

It is envisaged that consent from surgical clients to be interviewed and observed will be negotiated at the time of the first interview and will involve renegotiation at all subsequent contacts. Permission will be sought from surgical clients to review their case-notes (Appendix 4 [not reproduced]). Where surgical clients consent to being interviewed, either informally or formally, this will be recorded in the field diary or at the beginning of the tape where consent has been given to tape the interview. Surgical clients who consent to being informants will be told that they can withdraw from the research at any time and that their participation is strictly voluntary. They may therefore suspend either observation and/or interview at any such time they wish. At the first meeting, it will also be discussed with the client the possibility of a situation arising (e.g. where the client may be in pain) which results in them being unable to give verbal consent to the observation. The client can indicate their consent (or otherwise) to the continuing of the observation without verbal consent on the understanding that this will be written into the field notes of the researcher at the time and discussed with them at a later date. In seeking validation from the client of the observation, the client will be immediately informed that the care given by nursing and/or medical staff was observed at a time that they were unable to give verbal consent. If before or on reviewing the transcript of the observation the client wishes that the observation not be included in the study, all references to the observation will be deleted.

Protecting the privacy of informants will be of paramount concern, as will non-exploitation of any informant. At all times, the provision of any information collected and/or analysed will be communicated to informants as is reasonably practicable and especially prior to any publication of the study. Pseudonyms will be used when retrieving information from clients' case-notes.

Tapes, field data, and transcripts used in the research will be kept in secure storage at The University of South Australia for a period of seven years after the completion of the research and then disposed of according to NH&MRC guidelines.

8 Drugs

Not applicable.

9 Safety and ecological considerations

Not applicable: there are no issues of personal safety or ecological considerations associated with the research.

10 Analysis and reporting of results
10.1 Analysis

Following a procedure adapted from the works of Cheek and Rudge (1994), Kellehear (1993), Clark and Wheeler (1992) and Denzin (1989), the analysis will involve:

1. *Assembling of material.* As an ongoing process, all available material (review of the literature and documentation, observation notes, and interview transcripts) will be assembled together and read to acquire a sense of the data, its textual and contextual dimensions.
2. *Isolating issues, topics and themes.* In the reading, the aim is to illuminate what was being said, taken-for-granted assumptions, and what was missing or de-emphasized. Significant statements will be extracted, by both the researcher and informants, and the meaning of such observation and interview data checked with informants. The meaning of extracted statements will be formulated and organized into themes.
3. *Comparing different accounts.* Comparison of different accounts/elements/versions 'across and against each other' – a practice sometimes called 'intertextuality' (Game, 1991: 48; Cheek and Rudge, 1994) – will be done. Examination of 'deviant' accounts, with exceptions to patterned regularities, will be examined and checked with informants.
4. *Integrating all results.* Alternative interpretations will be advanced based upon the negative or deviant accounts and incorporated into a coherent descriptive text that attempts to deal with every instance of the focus under study (micro and macro levels). Validation of the descriptive results will be sought from informants.
5. *Moving from the descriptive into a critical discourse analysis.* Discourse analysis is a form of analysis that is attentive both to detail in text and context. It involves a careful reading of the descriptive text to elicit discursive patterns of meaning, contradictions and inconsistencies.

Discursive themes and subject positions will be forwarded and discussed within the framework of poststructuralist theory. In using discourse analysis, the researcher accepts that the descriptive text is not static, fixed and orderly, but rather is fragmented, inconsistent and contradictory (Gavey, 1989: 467).

6. *Reviewing the final analysis.* The final analysis will be returned to the informants to seek their input into their understanding of the results.

10.2 Reporting of the results

The results will be reported to the:

- Faculty of Nursing, The University of South Australia as a doctoral thesis.
- Organization and informants involved in the form of a written report.
- Nursing and medical professions by conference presentations and articles presented to appropriate journals for publication.

9.6   OTHER PROPOSALS IN THE LITERATURE

- Four 'specimen proposals' are included in the book by Locke et al. (2011). There is extensive and helpful editorial comment on each, and they cover a range of research approaches. The four proposals are:
  - ○ 'The effects of age, modality, complexity of response and practice on reaction time' (experimental design).
  - ○ 'Returning women students in the community college' (qualitative study).
  - ○ 'Teaching children to question what they read: an attempt to improve reading comprehension through training in a cognitive learning strategy' (quasi-experimental design).
  - ○ 'A competition strategy for worksite smoking cessation' (funded grant).

- Brink and Wood (1994: 255–375) include four sample research proposals, without editorial comment. The first two are descriptive studies, the third is a correlational study, and the fourth an experimental study. They are:
  - ○ 'Value orientations of Hutterian women in Canada'.
  - ○ 'Eating patterns successful dieters use to maintain weight loss'.
  - ○ 'The relationship between preterm infant sleep state disorganization and maternal–infant interaction'.
  - ○ 'Patient controlled analgesia for total hip arthroplasty patients'.

- Madsen (1983: 109–54) has two sample proposals, the first historical, the second experimental. They are:
  - ○ 'The Carnegie Institute of Washington, 1901–1904: Andrew Carnegie, Daniel Gilman and John Billings search for the exceptional man'.
  - ○ 'An investigation of two methods of achieving compliance with the severely handicapped in a classroom setting'.

- Maxwell (2012) reproduces, with commentary, a qualitative proposal entitled 'How basic science teachers help medical students learn: the students' perspective'.
- Maykut and Morehouse (1994: 165–77) include two shorter qualitative proposals, one on school climate, the other entitled 'An exploration of how children and adolescents with autism or autistic tendencies use facilitated communication in their lives'.
- Coley and Scheinberg (1990: 112–24) give the example, with critique, of a proposal for an intervention project where a community wants to address the problem of unintended adolescent pregnancy.
- Similarly, the proposal for an intervention project entitled 'A program to train interdisciplinary health care teams to work with the homeless' is presented and critiqued, as a case study, by Gitlin and Lyons (2008).
- Gilpatrick (1989) gives a progressive commentary and critique, throughout her book, of five intervention projects in a funding context. They are:

  o 'Education for parents of infants discharged from intensive care'.
  o 'Ambulance staff training in emergency medical services'.
  o 'City children involved in the arts community'.
  o 'Writing skills for retention of graduate students'.
  o 'Development of leadership by women of color in the antiviolence movement'.

- Wallen and Fraenkel (1991: 267–87) critique two student research proposals in education. They are: 'The effects of individualized reading upon student motivation in grade four' and 'The effects of a peer-counselling class on self esteem'.
- O'Donoghue and Haynes (1997: 91–169) give six examples of proposals in education, with these titles:

  o 'Goal directed behaviour, reputation enhancement and juvenile delinquency.'
  o 'The inclusion of children with a severe or profound intellectual disability in regular classrooms: How teachers manage the situation'.
  o 'Teacher of all the Gods: The educational thought of Ki Hajar Dewantara'.
  o 'An analysis of emergence, development and implementation of Italian as a school subject in the curriculum of Western Australian secondary schools over the period 1968 to 1994'.
  o 'Ideal algebra word problem test design: an application of the Rasch model for partial credit scoring'.
  o 'Language, thought and reality: A critical reassessment of the ideas of Benjamin Lee Whorf'.

Finally, we should note that there are now many examples of research proposals, from many different fields and areas of research, on the World Wide Web.

GLOSSARY

ACCOUNTING FOR VARIANCE   A central strategy in quantitative research; accounting for the variation in a dependent variable through studying its relationship with independent variables.

ACTION RESEARCH   Using empirical procedures, in iterative cycles of action and research, to solve practical problems.

AXIAL CODING   Discovering connections in the data between abstract concepts; used in grounded theory analysis; produces theoretical codes.

CASE STUDY   A research strategy which focuses on the in-depth, holistic and in-context study of one or more cases; will typically use multiple sources of data.

CODING   Placing labels or tags on pieces of qualitative data.

CONCEPTUAL FRAMEWORK   A framework showing the central concepts of a piece of research, and their conceptual status with respect to each other; often expressed as a diagram.

CORRELATION   A statistical technique for showing the strength and direction of the relationship between two variables. (KRT 12)

CORRELATIONAL SURVEY   A quantitative survey where the focus is on studying the relationships between variables.

DATA   The general term for observable information about, or direct experience of, some aspect of the world; see empirical, qualitative data, quantitative data.

DATA COLLECTION QUESTIONS   The actual questions asked to collect the data; examples are survey questions in quantitative research, and interview questions in qualitative research; data collection questions follow logically from specific research questions.

DEDUCTION   Moving downward in levels of abstraction, from more general and abstract to more specific and concrete; opposite of induction.

DEFINITIONS   A conceptual definition is the definition of a concept (or variable) in terms of other abstract concepts. This brings the need to find observable activities which are indicators of the concept; those activities constitute the operational definition of the concept. Construct validity is enhanced when there are tight logical links between the conceptual and operational definitions.

DELIBERATE SAMPLING   See purposive sampling.

DISCOURSE   A system of language which draws on a particular terminology and which encodes specific forms of knowledge; often used to refer to systems of knowledge and their associated practices.

EMPIRICAL   Based on direct experience or observation of the world.

EMPIRICAL CRITERION (FOR A RESEARCH QUESTION)   Is it clear what data are needed to answer this research question? If yes, the research question satisfies the empirical criterion. If no, further development of the research question is necessary.

EMPIRICISM   Philosophical term to describe the epistemological theory that sees experience as the foundation or source of knowledge.

ETHNOGRAPHY   The preferred research strategy of anthropologists; seeks to understand the symbolic significance of behaviour, in its cultural context, to the participants; aims for a full cultural description of the way of life of some group of people.

ETHNOMETHODOLOGY   Examines how people produce orderly social interaction in ordinary everyday situations; exposes the taken-for-granted 'rules' which constitute the infrastructure making everyday social interaction possible.

EXPERIMENT   A predominantly quantitative research design where: (1) one or more independent variables are manipulated to study their effect on a dependent variable; and (2) participants are randomly assigned to treatment or comparison groups.

FOCUS GROUP (INTERVIEW)   A powerful method of qualitative data collection where a small group of (six to eight) people are interviewed together.

GROUNDED THEORY   A distinctive strategy for research which aims to discover or generate explanatory theory grounded in data.

GROUNDED THEORY ANALYSIS   Specific procedures in the analysis of data for generating explanatory theory; focuses essentially on raising the conceptual level of (i.e. reconceptualizing) the data.

HIERARCHY OF CONCEPTS   A useful tool in planning and organizing research: area; topic; general research questions; specific research questions; data collection questions.

HYPOTHESIS   A predicted answer to a research question.

HYPOTHETICO-DEDUCTIVE MODEL   The central strategy of theory verification research which stresses the empirical testing of hypotheses deduced from theory. A hypothesis is developed from a theory by deduction and then tested against data.

INDUCTION Moving upwards in levels of abstraction, from more specific and concrete to more general and abstract; opposite of deduction.

INTERNAL VALIDITY OF A PROPOSAL Proposal as argument: the proposal should show strong internal consistency and coherence; all of its different parts should fit together. Especially, its methods should match its research questions; its argument and logic should be clear and consistent.

LATENT TRAIT The trait (or variable) we want to measure is hidden; we measure it by inference from its observable indicators.

MEASUREMENT The operation which turns data into numbers.

MIXED-METHOD RESEARCH Empirical research which brings together quantitative data (and methods) and qualitative data (and methods); there are many models for doing this.

MULTIVARIATE More than one dependent variable.

NATURALISTIC RESEARCH The social world is studied in its natural state, rather than contrived for research purposes.

OPEN CODING Concentrates on raising the conceptual level of the data. Guided by the question: what is this piece of data an example of? Used in grounded theory analysis; produces substantive codes.

PARADIGM A set of assumptions about the social world, and about what constitute proper techniques and topics for inquiring into that world; a set of basic beliefs, a world view, a view of how science should be done (ontology, epistemology, methodology).

PARTICIPANT OBSERVATION The preferred strategy for doing ethnography; the researcher aims to be both observer of and participant in the situation being studied, in order to understand it.

POPULATION The target group, usually large, about whom we want to develop knowledge, but which we cannot study directly; therefore we sample from that population.

POSITIVISM In a loose sense, this has come to mean an approach to social research that emphasizes the discovery of general laws, and separates facts from values; it often involves an empiricist commitment to naturalism and quantitative methods (Seale, 2011).

PRESTRUCTURED RESEARCH A research project with clear and specific research questions, a clear conceptual framework, a preplanned design and precoded data; see unfolding research.

PSYCHOMETRIC CHARACTERISTICS A general term referring to the measurement characteristics of a quantitative research instrument; usually includes reliability and validity.

PURPOSIVE (OR DELIBERATE) SAMPLING The sample is drawn from the population in a deliberate or targeted way, according to the logic of the research. Also known as deliberative sampling.

QUALITATIVE DATA Empirical information not in the form of numbers (most of the time, though not always, this means words).

QUALITATIVE RESEARCH Empirical research where the data are not in the form of numbers.

QUANTITATIVE DATA Empirical information in the form of numbers (or measurements).

QUANTITATIVE RESEARCH Empirical research where the data are in the form of numbers.

QUASI-EXPERIMENT Naturally occurring treatment groups permit comparisons between the groups approximating those of true experimental design.

REGRESSION A statistical technique for predicting scores on one variable from scores on another variable.

RELIABILITY (OF DATA) In quantitative research, the consistency of measurement: (1) consistency over time, i.e. test–retest reliability; and (2) consistency within indicators, i.e. internal consistency reliability. In qualitative research, the dependability of the data.

REPRESENTATIVE SAMPLING A sampling strategy where each unit of the population has an equal chance of being selected in the sample; directed at generalization.

RESEARCH QUESTIONS Organize the research by showing its purposes. General research questions guide the research by showing the general questions the research aims to answer; too general themselves to be answered directly; need to be made more specific. Specific research questions make the general research questions more specific; connect the general research questions to the data.

SAMPLE A smaller group which is actually studied, drawn from a larger population; data are collected (and analysed) from the sample, and inferences may then be made back to the population.

SECONDARY ANALYSIS The reanalysis of previously collected and analysed data.

SELECTIVE CODING Used in grounded theory analysis; identifies the core category of a grounded theory, and raises the conceptual level of the analysis a second time.

SEMIOTICS The science of signs; focuses on the process whereby something comes to stand for something else.

SOCIAL SCIENCE The scientific study of human behaviour; 'social' refers to people and their behaviour and to the fact that so much behaviour occurs in a social context; 'science' refers to the way that people and their behaviour are studied; see science as method.

STRUCTURED INTERVIEW Interview questions are pre-established and have preset response categories.

SURVEY A research strategy involving the collecting of data from a range of respondents (usually a sample drawn from a population); may be quantitative, qualitative, or mixed-method, depending on the nature of the data; usually involves a survey questionnaire.

THEORETICAL SAMPLING Consecutive cycles of data collection are guided by the theoretical directions emerging from the ongoing analysis; typically used in grounded theory research.

THEORETICAL SATURATION The 'end stage' of theoretical sampling in grounded theory research, when new data are not showing new theoretical elements, but rather confirming what has already been found.

THEORETICAL SENSITIVITY A term used in grounded theory; being alive and sensitive to the theoretical possibilities in the data; the ability to 'see', with theoretical and analytic depth, what is in the data.

THEORY Explanatory theory is a set of propositions which explain the data; the concepts in the propositions of the explanatory theory are more abstract than those in the data.

THEORY GENERATION RESEARCH Empirical research where the objective is discovering or constructing theory to explain data; starts with data, ends with theory.

THEORY VERIFICATION RESEARCH Empirical research where the objective is testing theory against data; starts with theory, uses data to test the theory (see hypothetico-deductive model).

TRIANGULATION Using several kinds of methods or data to study a topic; the most common type is data triangulation, where a study uses a variety of data sources.

UNFOLDING RESEARCH A research project where specific research questions are not clear in advance, a general approach rather than a tightly prefigured design is used, data are not prestructured; these things will unfold as the study progresses; see prestructured research.

UNSTRUCTURED INTERVIEW Interview questions and response categories are not pre-established; interview questions are deliberately open-ended.

VALIDITY A complex term with many meanings, both technical and general. Three important technical meanings are: the validity of a measuring instrument; the validity of a research design; the truth status of a research report.

REFERENCES

Alderson, P. and Morrow, V. (2011) *The Ethics of Research with Children and Young People: A Practical Handbook*. London: Sage.

Aspin, D.N. (1995) Logical empiricism, post-empiricism and education. In P. Higgs (ed.), *Metatheories in Philosophy of Education*, pp. 21–49. Johannesburg: Heinemann.

Bell, J. (2014) *Doing Your Research Project: A Guide for First-Time Researchers in Education and Social Science*, 6th edn. Maidenhead: Open University Press.

Bentham, J. (1823) *An Introduction to the Principles of Morals and Legislation*. London: W. Pickering and W. Wilson.

Bourdieu, P. (1973) Cultural reproduction and social reproduction. In R. Brown (ed.), *Knowledge, Education and Cultural Change*, pp. 71–112. London: Tavistock.

Brink, P.J. and Wood, M.J. (1994) *Basic Steps in Planning Nursing Research: From Question to Proposal*, 4th edn. Boston, MA: Jones and Bartlett.

Bryant, M.T. (2004) *The Portable Dissertation Advisor*. Beverly Hills, CA: Sage.

Bryman, A. (1988) *Quantity and Quality in Social Research*. London: Unwin Hyman.

Bryman, A. (1992) Quantitative and qualitative research: further reflections on their integration. In J.Brannen (ed.), *Mixing Methods: Qualitative and Quantitative Research*, pp. 57–78. Aldershot: Avebury.

Burgess, R.G. (1983) *Experiencing Comprehensive Education: A Study of Bishop McGregor School*. London: Methuen.

Burgess, R.G. (1989) Grey areas: Ethical dilemmas in educational ethnography. In R.G. Burgess (ed.), *The Ethics of Educational Research*, pp. 55–71. Lewes: Falmer Press.

Burton, S. and Steane, P. (eds) (2004) *Surviving Your Thesis*. London: Routledge.

Coley, S.M. and Scheinberg, C.A. (1990) *Proposal Writing*. Newbury Park, CA: Sage.

Creswell, J.W. (2013) *Research Design: Qualitative and Quantitative Approaches*, 4th edn. Thousand Oaks, CA: Sage.

Creswell, J.W. and Plano Clark, V. (2007) *Designing and Conducting Mixed Methods Research*. Thousand Oaks, CA: Sage.

Cryer, P. (2006) *The Research Student's Guide to Success*, 3rd edn. Maidenhead: Open University Press.

Denzin, N.K. (1997) *Interpretive Ethnography: Ethnographic Practices for the Twenty-First Century*. London: Sage.

Denzin, N.K. and Lincoln, Y.S. (eds) (2013) *The Sage Handbook of Qualitative Research,* 4th edn. Thousand Oaks, CA: Sage.

Dreher, M. (1994) Qualitative research methods from the reviewer's perspective. In J.M. Morse (ed.), *Critical Issues in Qualitative Research Methods*, pp. 281–97. Thousand Oaks, CA: Sage.

Edwards, R. and Mauthner, M (2002) Ethics and feminist research: theory and practice. In M. Mauthner, M. Birch, J. Jessop and T. Miller (eds), *Ethics in Qualitative Research*, pp. 14–31. London: Sage.

Eisner, E.W. (1991) *The Enlightened Eye: Qualitative Inquiry and the Enhancement of Educational Practice*. New York: Macmillan.

Elwell, F. (1996) *Verstehen: The Sociology of Max Weber*.

Eynon, R., Fry, J. and Schroeder, R. (2008) The ethics of internet research. In N.G. Fielding, R.M. Lee and G. Blank (eds), *The Sage Handbook of Online Research Methods*, pp. 23–41. London: Sage.

Frankena, W. (1973) *Ethics*. Englewood Cliffs, NJ: Prentice Hall.

Gill, J. and Johnson, P. (2011) *Research Methods for Managers*, 4th edn. London: Sage.

Gilpatrick, E. (1989) *Grants for Nonprofit Organizations: A Guide to Funding and Grant Writing*. New York: Praeger.

Gitlin, L.N. and Lyons, K.J. (2008) *Successful Grant Writing*, 3rd edn. New York: Springer.

Glaser, B. (1992) *Basics of Grounded Theory Analysis*. Mill Valley, CA: Sociology Press.

Gomm, R. (2004) Research ethics. In *Social Research Methodology: A Critical Introduction*, pp. 298–322. Basingstoke: Palgrave Macmillan.

Hammersley, M. (1992) Deconstructing the qualitative–quantitative divide. In J. Brannen (ed.), *Mixing Methods: Qualitative and Quantitative Research*, pp. 39–55. Aldershot: Avebury.

Hammersley, M. and Traianou, A. (2012) *Ethics in Qualitative Research*. Thousand Oaks, CA: Sage.

Higgs, P. (1995) Metatheories in philosophy of education: Introductory overview. In P. Higgs (ed.), *Metatheories in Philosophy of Education*, pp. 3–17. Johannesburg: Heinemann.

Holmes, R.M. (1998) *Fieldwork with Children*. London: Sage.

Homan, R. (2004) The principle of assumed consent: The ethics of gatekeeping. In M. McNamee and D. Bridges (eds), *The Ethics of Educational Research*, pp. 23–40. Oxford: Blackwell.

Janesick, V.J. (1994) The dance of qualitative research design: Metaphor, methodolatry, and meaning. In N.K. Denzin and Y.S. Lincoln (eds), *Handbook of Qualitative Research*, pp. 209–19. Thousand Oaks, CA: Sage.

Jones, C. (2011) Ethical issues in online research. British Educational Research Association on-line resource. https://www.bera.ac.uk/wp-content/uploads/2014/03/Ethical-issues-in-online-research.pdf (accessed 24 August 2015).

Kant, I. (1964) *Groundwork to the Metaphysics of Morals*. London: Routledge.

Kelly, M. (2012) Research questions and proposals. In C. Seale (ed.), *Researching Society and Culture*, 3rd edn, pp. 97–117. London: Sage.

Krathwohl, D.R. (1998) *Methods of Educational and Social Science Research: An Integrated Approach*. New York: Longman.

Lauffer, A. (1983) *Grantsmanship*, 2nd edn. Beverly Hills, CA: Sage.

Lauffer, A. (1984) *Grantsmanship and Fundraising*. Beverly Hills, CA: Sage.

Le Voi, M. (2002) Responsibilities, rights and ethics. In S. Potter (ed.), *Doing Postgraduate Research*, pp. 153–164. London: Sage.

Lefferts, R. (1982) *Getting a Grant in the 1980s*, 2nd edn. Englewood Cliffs, NJ: Prentice Hall.

Locke, L.F., Spirduso, W.W. and Silverman, S.J. (2011) *Proposals that Work*, 6th edn. Thousand Oaks, CA: Sage.

Madsen, D. (1983) *Successful Dissertations and Theses: A Guide to Graduate Student Research from Proposal to Completion*. San Francisco, CA: Jossey-Bass.

Marshall, C. and Rossman, G.B. (2015) *Designing Qualitative Research*, 6th edn. Thousand Oaks, CA: Sage.

Marshall, S. and Green, N. (2010) *Your PhD Companion*, 3rd edn. Oxford: How to Books.

Maxwell, J.A. (2012) *Qualitative Research Design: An Interactive Approach*, 3rd edn. Thousand Oaks, CA: Sage.

Maykut, P. and Morehouse, R. (1994) *Beginning Qualitative Research: A Philosophic and Practical Guide*. London: Falmer.

McNamee, M. and Bridges, D. (eds) (2002) *The Ethics of Educational Research*. Oxford: Blackwell.

Meador, R. (1991) *Guidelines for Preparing Proposals*, 2nd edn. Chelsea, MI: Lewis.

Miles, M.B., Huberman, A.M. and Saldaña, J. (2014) *Qualitative Data Analysis*, 3rd edn. Thousand Oaks, CA: Sage.

Milgram, S. (1974) *Obedience to Authority*. New York: Harper and Row.

Mill, J. S. (1863) *Utilitarianism*. London: Parker, Son and Bourn.

Miner, L.E. and Griffith, J. (1993) *Proposal Planning and Writing*. Phoenix, AZ: Oryx.

Morse, J.M. (2013) What is qualitative health research? In N.K. Denzin and Y.S. Lincoln (eds), *The Sage Handbook of Qualitative Research*, 4th edn, pp. 401–414. Thousand Oaks, CA: Sage.

Nathan, R. (2005a) An anthropologist goes under cover. *The Chronicle of Higher Education*, 29 July.

Nathan, R. (2005b) *My Freshman Year: What a Professor Learned by Becoming a Student*. Ithaca, NY: Cornell University Press.

Neumann, W.L. (1994) *Social Research Methods: Qualitative and Quantitative Approaches*, 2nd edn. Boston: Allyn & Bacon.

O'Donoghue, T. (2007) *Planning Your Qualitative Research Project: An Introduction to Interpretivist Research in Education*. Abingdon: Routledge.

O'Donoghue, T. and Haynes, F. (1997) *Preparing Your Thesis/Dissertation in Education: Comprehensive Guidelines*. Katoomba, NSW: Social Science Press.

Pendlebury, S. and Enslin, P. (2001) Representation, identification and trust: Towards and ethics of educational research. *Journal of Philosophy of Education,* 35(3), 361–70.

Pring, R. (2004) *Philosophy of Educational Research*, 2nd edn. London: Continuum.

Punch, K. (2011) *Introduction to Social Research*, 3rd edn. London: Sage.

Punch, M. (1994) Politics and ethics in qualitative research. In N.K. Denzin and Y.S. Lincoln (eds), *Handbook of Qualitative Research,* pp. 83–97. Thousand Oaks, Ca: Sage.

Rosenberg, M. (1968) *The Logic of Survey Analysis*. New York: Basic Books.

Rudestam, K.E. and Newton, R.R. (2014) *Surviving Your Dissertation*, 4th edn. London: Sage.

Schumacher, D. (1992) *Get Funded!* Newbury Park, CA: Sage.

Seale, C. (ed.) (2011) *Researching Society and Culture*, 3rd edn. London: Sage.

Sikes, P. and Piper, H. (2010) 'A courageous proposal, but … this would be a high risk study': Ethics review procedures, risk and censorship. In *Researching Sex and Lies in the Classroom: Allegations of Sexual Misconduct in Schools,* pp. 24–34. Abingdon: Routledge.

Simons, H. (2009a) Whose data are they? Ethics in case study research. In *Case Study Research in Practice,* pp. 96–111. London: Sage.

Simons, H. (2009b) *Case Study Research in Practice*. London: Sage.

Snee, H. (2010) Using Blog Analysis. NCRM Realities Toolkit 10. http://eprints.ncrm.ac.uk/1321/2/10-toolkit-blog-analysis.pdf.

Steane, P. (2004) Ethical issues in research. In S. Burton and P. Steane (eds), *Surviving Your Thesis,* pp. 59–70. London: Routledge.

Strunk, W., Jr and White, E.B. (2000) *The Elements of Style*, 4th edn. Boston, MA: Allyn & Bacon.

Tashakkori, A. and Teddlie, C. (2010) *Handbook of Mixed Methods in Social and Behavioural Research*, 2nd edn. Thousand Oaks, CA: Sage.

Thomson, P. (ed.) *Doing Visual Research with Children and Young People*. Abingdon: Routledge.

Tonkiss, F. (2011) Analyzing discourse. In C. Seale (ed.), *Researching Society and Culture,* 3rd edn, pp. 227–44. London: Sage.

Tornquist, E.M. (1993) *From Proposal to Publication: An Informal Guide to Writing about Nursing Research*. San Francisco, CA: Addison-Wesley.

Walford, G. (2005) Research ethical guidelines and anonymity. *International Journal of Research and Method in Education,* 28(1), 83–93.

Wallen, N.E. and Fraenkel, J.R. (1991) *Educational Research: A Guide to the Process*. New York: McGraw-Hill.

Ward, A. (2002) The writing process. In S. Potter (ed.), *Doing Postgraduate Research*, pp. 71–116. London: Sage.

Wiles, R., Prosser, J., Bagnoli, A., Clark, A., Davies, K., Holland, S. and Renold, E. (2008) *Visual Ethics: Ethical Issues in Visual Research*. ESRC National Centre for Research Methods Review Paper. Southampton: NCRM. http://eprints.ncrm.ac.uk/421/1/MethodsReviewPaperNCRM-011.pdf (accessed 24 August 2015).

INDEX